CONNE

Happiness is an inside job. Let *Connect* show you how to take action, push past fears and gain courage, so you can live the life you've been dreaming of.

JACK CANFIELD, Coauthor of the *Chicken Soup for the Soul®* and *The Success Principles™*

Letting go isn't giving up; it's understanding that the best is yet to come. Let *Connect* show you how to learn from your past, take back your power, and truly live like you have never lived before.

MIKE DOOLEY, *NY Times* bestselling author of *Infinite Possibilities*

Dawn Burnett is shining a light on the practices of mindset that make a rich, joy filled, thrilling life possible. Each of us has to tap in and "Connect" in order to make our blue sky dreams come true.

SHERI SALATA, Chief Visionary and Co-Host of *This is Fifty with Sheri + Nancy*

Over the years that I have connected with Dawn, I have watched her blossom as a writer and a human being. She has embodied the ancient secrets of Self-knowing and Self-love and has made it a part of her relationship teachings. *Connect* acts like a light on the path for anyone who has experienced separation from love. Dawn's insightful writings demonstrate her evolution through a direct personal experience of how she has used her divorce as a powerful medium to break through the time-bound psycho-somatic barriers, which often hold people back from good health and happiness.

GURUDEV SHRI AMRITJI- The first Yoga Guru who brought the Inner Dimension of Patanjali's Ashtanga Yoga to the West, 1960

CONNECT

CONNECT

How to Love and Accept
Yourself After Divorce

Dawn Burnett

Clovercroft Publishing

Connect: How to Love and Accept Yourself After Divorce

©2018 by Dawn Burnett

Published by Clovercroft Publishing, Franklin, Tennessee

Cover and Interior Design by Suzanne Lawing

Edited by Lapiz Digital Services

Printed in the United States of America

978-1-94848412-1

CONTENTS

FOREWORD

The one thing

Anyone who has ever been through a divorce has been thrust into the tornado of emotional turmoil. It eats you up, swirls you around, and destroys your household. A divorce resembles a natural disaster. Only after the dust has settled, we can claim what we have left. Sometimes we only have the rubble and the foundation, and that's enough. Yet it's truly hard and maybe even impossible to see at the time. How will I survive this life? How will I overcome?

One path to success is giving back.

Giving is living and it allows us to connect with our higher purpose. It takes our minds off of distraction and instead focuses on hope. Dawn Burnett wrote this book to give the gift of healing to the world. She's traveled the path through destruction and has walked the talk as a single mom. She's been through the rough stuff and continues along the journey of enlightenment with you.

If you live in Tornado alley like some of my friends do, you know that a tornado weaves a long path of destruction, leaving the ruins of shattered houses and lives in its wake. There are television reports of buses, trees, and couches swirling high in the air. For just a brief moment, there's a haunting sound. Many people report hearing the sounds of a mysterious eerie train, and complete darkness.

In the hours and days following the event, people are

rescued. Parents venture out of their shelters, cradling their young, covering and shielding the children while they venture out. They open the doors from the cold damp ground, where they'd been hiding to survey the wreckage.

And the wreckage is extreme.

As they survey the landscape, they see evidence of lives lost. Families shifted and separated forever. Homes were torn to the ground. This is the way a divorce can feel. Yet when the shock of the tornado clears, in the days and weeks to come, there's also surprise. I worked the Joplin tornado and nothing prepared me for seeing mansions (no, not trailer parks) decimated to the ground.

The news reports seemed to focus on feeble housing structures or impoverished areas yet when we pulled into Joplin, the devastation was remarkable and the destruction was not limited to a specific class of people. The streets were silent yet there were expensive crystal objects, books, and even food sitting on countertops in the midst of a destruction. Walking down the street felt like you were a zombie in a scene from the book of Eli.

This is how it is with divorce.

I had taken my young boys there to show them how to give back. It was spring break. Yet walking down the street sadness enveloped my heart. I could see the loss on their faces as they read the words spray painted on the houses.

Here!

Seeing those words meant they were alive.

And on another boarded up the house,

I love you Dad. Goodbye.

With each step, we could see who survived and who didn't. And in divorce, it's the same way. Some people survive better than others. Some take one step forward and two steps back.

In my journey to give back to others on a spring break mission trip instead of allowing the kids to be super consumers, I discovered the truth.

The pure weight of giving back to all of these lives transformed would certainly transform our own.

I learned that giving away means to truly give a piece of your heart. I've been permanently damaged by giving, whether it was my time working as an airplane crisis team leader in the aftermath of a crash or visiting a nursing home. I've felt and witnessed a lot of tragedy, including divorce. I have seen one partner heal, and one partner spiral downward into the darkness, allowing the event to permanently change them. After my dad's own wife left him, he committed suicide.

Has any child been more impacted by divorce than me?

Of course, they have.

Yet divorce feels isolating.

And it is, but only for a while.

Only if you stay beneath the rubble. Today, world changer, it's your choice.

Your choice to make.

In Joplin, we saw the destruction. But we also saw something else, Hope.

We saw resilience unlike any other. We saw a warrior spirit! We saw a positive energy that connected each and every human at their core.

As we walked with burdened and shattered hearts, we got halfway down the street and we began to see the healing. Words of inspiration began to appear.

Joy!

And yet another,

We will rise up!

And finally, on one completely battered home without a

roof,

Never give up.

Someone had scrawled this on what was left of the front of the house, held together with plywood.

My friend, there's beauty in the ashes and Dawn and all of the other contributors here in this book show you why. Read the stories in this valuable book. In your journey to healing, I encourage you, never give up.

Life will eventually be beautiful again. The sun will usher out the rain.

As you journey through these stories, take one step and then another. There's an unimaginable joy on the road ahead.

—Tammy Kling

Tammy Kling is the founder of OnFire books, the creator of the best-selling book The Compass, founder of "The Conversation" event, and a TEDx speaker on the topic of the power of words. She is a regular leadership speaker at Pepsi, Mary Kay, and other large companies on communication.

INTRODUCTION

Why do relationships fail?

We are taught in life: grow up, get a job, and then get married, but nobody really coaches us on what a good marriage looks like or what's required to have a successful marriage. Instead, we lead with our minds and what feels and looks good to us, our conditioned belief that love is obtained through others, when in reality unless we find love within, we will never find love outside. We go searching for love, approval, and acceptance outside of self and this eventually leaves us feeling bankrupt. That's because we have been sold a false bill of goods, and we wonder why over 50% of marriages in the U.S. end in divorce.

How many times have you read in the tabloids that a marriage breaks up due to infidelity? Yes, that is a legitimate reason for a relationship to fail but what's overlooked is the root cause driving the choice for infidelity. Usually, when you peel back all the layers and dig deep in pursuit of the truth, the act stems back to childhood. A false belief system about self, a lack of respect or confused perception of value; these hidden trapped emotions when left uncovered and not dealt with can cause havoc to any relationship.

Let's examine the case of a child who grew up in a verbally abusive home. The child was told over and over that they weren't good enough, they then internalize that the experience is stored in their cellular memory bank and without even realizing the long-term effects that child grows up, gets married, and attracts a partner which displays disrespect to them; a reflection of where they are at with themselves and before you know it the relationship is filled with toxicity. The inability to communicate effectively grows and resentment builds. Their partner doesn't feel valued because they have never learned to value and love themselves first. One of them becomes frustrated, meets someone else whom they feel values them more than their partner, one thing leads to another and before you know it, infidelity is suffocating their relationship. This is one of the tipping points that lead to divorce.

From there, the biggest remnant that follows the divorce is the need to find oneself, learning how to love and accept oneself during a time of upheaval. So where do you start? Is it possible to restore and resurrect from disaster? The answer is, "YES." However, healing will require work and commitment on your part. But this is your chance to finally achieve self-acceptance, remove the masks you've been wearing and lay down all the hurts of the past that you've been carrying around. A time to break free from your conditioned thinking, an opportunity to connect within and uncover the superhero you've been designed to be. A time to turn in your victim card all while knowing that I am here for you and so are all the other authors in this book. We'll help guide you on what to expect and mentor you so you can thrive instead of cry, exchanging beauty for ashes.

Chapter 1

LEARNING TO LOVE SELF

"The obstacles in our path are not blocking us; they are redirecting us. Their purpose is not to interfere with our happiness; it is to point us toward new routes to our happiness, new possibilities, new doorways."

— Barbara De Angelis

Life is a journey and our conditioned minds can keep us trapped in a whirlwind of dysfunction. I know, I was that person. I had to learn how to shape my attention and channel my energy; how to stop repeating my relational patterns. It's a self- discovery process that is all about returning to the source within. Often times what we are seeking from objects and people outside of ourselves is what we already have within; it's all about refining and self-discovery. This was a wake-up call, but in the end, I stopped trying the impossible, filling my ego, which was an insatiable void. This knowledge will catapult your awakening and help you understand your ego mind and self. I want to help you progress in life so you stop looking outside of yourself and start looking from within. When we reject ourselves, it's like putting on a tourniquet, cutting ourselves off from our higher self at a root level. So I want to encourage you to accept yourself at this moment exactly as who you are, because it's your time to experience true love.

When you are not looking for love, love comes to you; when you run after it, it runs from you, so it's time to stop looking for others to fill your void, heal your insecurities that stem from your past and unleash the super YOU, just as I have. Embody the advice in these chapters instead of just intellectually understanding it. Your search should be within and not from outside. Accept yourself with gratitude just exactly as you are, it's time to stop beating yourself up and putting yourself down, because you were born with a greater awareness.

This is your opportunity to make a shift from your past to expanding your consciousness, it's your chance to choose to process things differently which is what automatically happens when you operate in consciousness. A time to go inside and connect with self at a much deeper level, it's never about changing others, it's always about changing self for when you do the world around you changes, after all the only people we control in life our ourselves. When you change in this way, you will advance in healing and then when hardship comes you won't feel depressed or be sent in a downward spiral. You will recognize truth and connect from within at a higher level of consciousness. So how have I learned this? There have been many teachers along the way but the one who has impacted my life the most is Guru Shri Amritji.

How Did I Get Here?

Now you may be wondering the same thing, how did you end up divorced? From the moment, we are proposed to, the time the ring is placed on our finger, we never think, "will this be forever?" On the contrary, we say, "Until death does us part." Divorce was never the plan but it is in some peoples' minds the end. I am here to encourage you that it can be the beginning, of a beautiful thriving and flourishing life but the choice at the end of the day starts and ends with you. I had to quickly come to the same realization as I took ownership for my part of a passing marriage as I dealt with my past junk and gained the courage to heal. My prayer is that you will be inspired by my story and if it's just one life that I'm able to empower for the choice to change, then the pain I have transformed to my platform was worth it all.

Beauty for Ashes

My life wasn't always happy, not at all! So what's my story? I believe it all starts back from when I was a kid, what I saw, learned, and heard.

I am from a broken home, one of five kids. Life was very confusing as a kid, my parents seemed to fight all the time and I don't remember chunks of my childhood, my mind has a way of trying to protect me, a way of blocking out the pain. My father was abusive toward my mother, and according to the story, we were told she was the one in the wrong, something about unfaithful. But as I grew older I realized that it takes 2 to tango, and no matter what the situation in life is nobody deserves to be abused! There were many scary moments in that house. Thinking back, I remember one day my Dad got mad, karate chopped the table and the Halloween candy flew everywhere. Run and hide is what you think of first as a child. Hiding is what I learned to do very well. I too was abused as a child but not from my father, it was a confused and fragmented family member. Now I tell you this because the foundation determines our future when not addressed and healed. Mine of course was not healed. Despite my father being a better man today and my Mom passing away and transitioning to heaven with angel wings, there is residue that was left behind. Some of which I was not even aware of.

As I graduated from high school and college, I married my childhood sweetheart. Although he was a good man, he was best for someone else. We married as soon as I turned 21 and we were more like brother and sister than lovers. I wanted more out of life and he was content remaining as he was. So like I had seen my parents do, I left my ex in pursuit of something better, or so I thought he was. My first husband was my escape hatch, a release from the turmoiled home I had been raised in and when I left him I bounced. Right from a home into the fire is the best way I can describe marriage number 2. I didn't take time to work on myself and understand how I played my part in failing the marriage, I was too busy trying to fill my EGO; the insatiable void. When we do this, we create the same patterns if not worse and that's exactly what I just created, I married what I had witnessed in my father, despite loving both men, I stepped into more abuse.

It was registered in my body that's right; our body has coding and when past experiences and beliefs are laid as a childhood foundation unless they are reprogrammed that's what we seek.

I hardly knew my second husband. I remember working for a travel company and I was stationed to work with the British visitors in Orlando, FL, so I grew quite fond of them. So fond that one day I decided to fly to the Jersey Channel Islands and track down an old friend. I was 23 at the time; I packed up my suitcase and flew to a place I had never dreamed of going prior too. I remember picking up a phone book while I was there and calling several different people trying to track down my friend Veronica. That, of course, led me to great success, as someone had heard of Veronica and said they would track her down. The next day, I heard a knock at my hotel door, as I flung it open there stood Veronica with a dozen red roses insisting that I come to stay the remaining trip with her. I wasn't grown and mature and the time spent was not as connected as it could have been but I'm happy to say we still are connected to this day.

When I left the Jersey Channel Islands, I flew over to London where I tracked down another friend who was attending Guildford University and that led me to a fun evening out. Being the lost soul that I was, when my friends decided to retire for the evening I decided to carry on with more fun by myself in a place I was not familiar with. I headed back to the hotel, asked the gentleman at the front desk where I could go out as a New Yorker by myself and feel safe, his response was, "You can go out anywhere around here and feel safe, we don't carry guns." That was 25 years ago and of course, a lot has changed in the world today. Looking back I think what bravery I had or was it stupidity. Well, that trip out to the nightclub cost me fifteen and half years, as the years to follow were filled with an immense amount of turmoil. Yes, I met someone and instantly fell for him; Nathan was quite the dapper man, filled with charm. What I didn't realize is that charmers are abusers in many cases.

Nathan and I spent 3 amazing days together before I flew home and he won me over. But the ink on my divorce papers from Sam wasn't even completely dry. I didn't care though, I was in my early 20s and nobody could tell me otherwise, this was the man for me, there was no reasoning. When we want something bad enough, we find a way of making it happen. That's exactly what I did. I flew over to England and got married to Nathan but our life got turned upside down from the moment we said, "I, do." It's so important to watch for the red flags, the signs that God and the Universe deliver to tell us we are off course. If only I knew then what I know today, I would have let Nathan go. But no, I was in love or at least I thought I was. Upon returning to the U.S., Nathan was detained and deported. I thought, "How could this happen? Did someone tip off immigration? I even went to the INS to make sure we had the correct paperwork." None of that mattered, the reality is I had to fly back and get this man back in the country or say goodbye and after all, I had already been through to get him into the country, I wasn't giving up now.

I sold almost everything including my house back to my ex-husband, I quit my job, took my two, 45-pound suitcases and headed to England. With as many challenges as I had already conquered in my life, I felt I was destined to succeed. I did 6 months later as I had it out with a worker at the U.S. embassy in London until we received the correct visa. Finally, Nathan and I were going home, well to the new home that we were about to establish.

Those 15 and a half years were the most challenging years of my life! I had just attracted the reflection of toxicity into my life at the level of where I was at on the inside but didn't understand it or recognize it at the time. There is no way our marriage had a fighting chance because we were 2 halves not wholes from the start. The foundation was knowing each other 2 weeks before we got married, meeting each other when we were both still in a relationship with other people and immigration issues on top of that. With that kind of pressure, it's enough to make anyone crack, oh and he did but through the insecurities of my past we were like oil and water. Adding to the mix, we were living with my sister until we could get enough money together to buy a house as I had just burned through my entire life savings of $17,000 to get Nathan back in the country. My grandfather was so mad at me that he wouldn't speak to me for six months. Everything about this marriage was wrong.

So why did we stick it out? We were both stubborn people who couldn't let our Egos lose. Instead, it was our sanity that was lost. We moved forward with the relationship and in less than one year I got pregnant with our daughter Tiffany whom I wanted really bad. Ask and you shall receive, just make sure you are ready for what you ask for. We brought a child into a toxic relationship so naturally, Tiffany even inside of the womb was fussy and colicky. We learned the ropes of being what we felt were good parents, we bought a house and both became established in our jobs. We put on the front of being a happy couple and worked really hard to keep up with the Jones from a 3,500 square feet home to fancy cars and trips. Our clothes matched our egos and we looked to others like we had it all when in reality we were both a mess.

Tiffany took dance classes, went to a private school and her clothes were beautiful. She was my pride and joy but due to the toxicity in the house, she didn't grow up with the inner joy that she well deserved. Over time, the verbal abuse in our household became so bad I was in and out of almost every hospital in Central Florida. Despite going to church every week and putting on a facade, our marriage wasn't working. My life, marriage, and health were a train wreck. I did the best I could to hold it together because it was the "Christian" thing to do. Getting divorced was not an option; I had to do every-thing I could to keep our marriage together. I read books, went to counseling, and medicated myself with shopping which amounted to a pile of debt. I worked out hard and submerged myself in my daughter and work. What I didn't realize is my inner being was suffering so bad that I was killing myself.

It wasn't until my son Conner was born that I woke up and realized that there was a trend in going to hospitals every year to experiencing near death car crashes. The toxic environment was attracting more and more toxicity in my life. Why in the world did I decide to have the church pray for me to have another child when doctors told me it was impossible and my relationship was a mess? Because I wanted a boy and guess what, my treasure Conner is the best gift that was ever given. I decided to do almost everything different with my son than I did with my daughter. I took time off work to raise him in his first year; I ate healthy, sang to him and used essential oils each night to provide him with a calm environment. Well, there is no amount of oil that will fix a house full of vulgar language and slamming doors through walls. Yes, that's the level the abuse in our house had arisen to.

I nearly died having Conner as he was born C-Section and the doctor never came to visit me post delivery, leaving me with bandages that caused an infection and when removed took my skin right with it. But despite not being able to move out of bed or being able to hold Conner for the first 2 weeks I vowed to not let anything derail his life.

At the age of 2, Conner got a compromised immune system due to vaccinations that led me to a popular children's hospital where they wanted to remove body parts. Our natural doctor had pronounced Conner with severe Celiac disease, and it was the moment that led me to the most profound change in my life which later went on to save both of our lives. That's right I went back to college to get my degree in Alternative Medicine. It's through my University studies where I learned about mind/body connection and how our thoughts are stored at a cellular level and when negative they affect our DNA and create disease. Suddenly, I started to connect all of the dots. This was the reason why I kept ending up in hospitals every year; I was drenched in toxicity, with nowhere to turn but out.

One day I remember Nathan came home and we were arguing over a paper for our rental property, suddenly Nathan grabbed me by the throat and pinned me up against the wall right in front of our children. Conner was 3 at the time and Tiffany was 12. That was the straw that broke the camel's back. While Nathan was away on a business trip, my father was in town from New York visiting with my stepmom and they both said, "It's time to get out." I remember saying to my Dad, "I am scared he will come after me." My dad assured me everything would work out OK and it did. I left Nathan, it was April 2009, I remember it like yesterday as it was my daughter's birthday and we were in hiding at a hotel, Nathan showed up only to try and con me into getting back together. But it was at that moment I started to see clearly, think differently and stood my ground.

In June of 2009, we were divorced, and in July, I packed up three 26 ft Penske trucks, two kids, and a dog and headed to Upstate NY, near Syracuse to a place where I knew nobody because I felt God was leading me there and it was an opportunity to heal and deal. My family lived within 1–3 hours away and I could now finally take a breather. Was I scared? You bet I was, but nothing could be scarier than having a man's hands around your throat being pinned up against a wall.

There were challenges that came and there were two that stood out the most. Tiffany was now a teenager and with it came the play between both parents when Nathan picked them up once a month on the weekend, and the attitude that came with it. My baby girl was slipping away and all I could do was fight. But if that wasn't bad enough on October 30, 2009, Conner and I were on our way to pick up Tiffany, she had just landed captain of the cheerleading squad, she was at a cheerleading's Mom's house of whom I had not met. We were waiting to turn when from behind I heard a loud bang and it was lights out. Conner and I had been plowed into the ground by a hit and run drunk driver, pushing us into oncoming traffic. I lost track of time and space as I felt myself floating in the dark from what appeared to be another dimension. It was a female voice that I did not recognize that brought me back and from there I realized I could barely move, that I had a son and I was in traffic. The voice guided me to line my vehicle up in my lane and my van never worked again. I got out of the van with the help of an amazing female citizen and jimmied the door open a crack to get my son out, running in front of oncoming traffic with my boy for safety, I collapsed on the side of the road, that's what a rush of adrenaline does to us. From there, paramedics arrived, loaded us on body boards and into the ambulance. My phone thanks to the tough cover it had which was still working, rang and the paramedic picked it up. My daughter was on the other line and because his son played ball with the Cheerleading Mom's son, my daughter was guided to where we were.

I remember I was on the biggest spiritual high of my life and suddenly my purpose became crystal clear, to take all that I have learned in college and life and spread it to the world. That's exactly the reason for writing this book.

I was one course away from graduating and I could barely move my arms. My daughter had a cheerleading competition and the NY school was fighting me against my son's FL medical exemption letter towards vaccinations. But there was no getting me down, I just survived one of the biggest mishaps in my history, there is a clear reason as to why I was left to live. We had also discovered the day after the crash that my son's seat had broken right out of the floor and he walked away without an outer scratch which later landed me a spot on TBN to share my story. With every ounce of my being, I fought and I fought hard with courage, dedication, and perseverance and I graduated Summa Cum Laude 4.0 and completely reversed my son's health. Saved and healed my own life and had awakened to a new world, the one I saw through my new set of lenses.

I would not trade any of my experiences good nor bad for anything, they have molded and shaped me into what I am today. Has it been tough? Oh, you bet it has, but for every bit of challenge and toughness, there have been four to five amazing miracles and magical moments. I can honestly say I have lived the best nine years of my life through being divorced.

Now, I'm not encouraging nor promoting divorce in any way but I am here to inspire and empower you so that if you are going through a divorce whether by choice or not or you have been divorced for a while, there is an amazing side to life that is ahead for all of us if we seek it.

So what happened during those nine years? I graduated from the University in March 2010 and my mom dropped dead with no warning just 6 weeks later that could have turned my life upside down but in honor of her bravery and courage as an abused divorced in the past woman, I vowed to go on to do great things and keep the legacy of bravery alive. I moved in August 2010 to New Jersey, just 45 minutes outside of NYC, my dream since I was a little girl. There we made an amazing home for ourselves for a year and during that time my son got contracted at the age of 6 with Stewart Talent in NYC. I wrote my first book *True Confessions of the Heart* and got picked from the audience for an appearance on Dr. Oz, and I was chosen for the *Ambush Make Over* on The Today Show. I worked on a TV show pilot with a former business partner, former only due to a rare heart disease that took her precious life within less than a year of our filming. I traveled to Los Angeles and connected with some amazing people in the media and shortly after that I moved back to FL to be with my sister who was left standing on her own.

Tiffany, Conner, our dog Mitzi, and I made a great home for ourselves in Orlando, August 2011, and I went on to connect with more people in the media. I could not do anything to remove the inner passion inside of me. More turmoil came as Tiffany staged a leave with her Dad and when it was time for Conner and Tiffany to return only Conner showed up. Tiffany remained in Georgia and it was another really tough hurdle to get over but the only other choice was to crumble. Tiffany remained with Nathan for her senior year and I had no contact with her until she graduated. I was blessed to see her walk the stage and then she moved to Orlando where I got to spend a year with her, indulging in all of the parental excitement from car shopping to apartment shopping and college sign on. I felt as if I hadn't missed a beat. In reality, I had missed an entire year but I made a decision at that moment to shift my focus on the positive instead of the negative as I knew if I were going to succeed in life I couldn't afford the luxury of a negative thought.

Conner continued to grow and we walked through many hurdles of him being bullied in elementary school because he was small for his age. But as the saying goes, don't mess with mama bear. I fought the school and Conner continued to grow to learn that although words have currency, they only define us when we choose to let them. Conner continued in acting and music, and it is so beautiful to see him grow. He is now 14 years old and the best treasure a Mom could ever ask for.

Tiffany, on the other hand, decided to move back to GA and now VA where she continues to run her own race in her own lane and that's OK. Tiffany is an adult now and life is a classroom. As a parent, I have learned, sometimes the hard way that our kids are on loaner to us, we are here to teach and at the end of the day, they are the real keepers of their own lives and we are blessed by God to have them as a gift.

As for me, I have had the amazing opportunity of extensive travel from the red carpet in Hollywood, box seats at the Macy's Day Parade, Multi private parties and VIP passes for the ball drop in NYC, private viewing for the tree lighting ceremony in the city, to the Espy Awards in Los Angeles and sipping on champagne in the Plaza Hotel just to name a few. I got to co-author with Jack Canfield, publish the *Connect* series, accept acting gigs, write four songs and work with some of the most talented artists and producers. I made TV and radio appearances, hosted my own radio show and interviewed some of the most amazing authors and gurus. I accepted speaking engagements, aligned with my University, became a contributing writer for Huff Post and Arianna Huffington's Thrive Global. I am founder of *A New Dawn Natural Solutions,* co-inventor of *Cami-Soul* and now joined by amazing co-authors for this book, some of the most courageous and brilliant women and men an author could choose to align with. My life is truly blessed and I am grateful that I had another shot at life to see it all unfold.

Everything has unfolded in my life exactly as it is supposed to since the divorce, in the perfect order of my willingness to be taught and transformed. Step by step, year by year, turning my ashes into inner beauty, the kind no amount of money can buy. The realization that each experience of my relationships was basically related to my relationship with self. The understanding is that nobody can love me any better than I can love myself, a great life lesson that love dissolves borders and it all starts and ends with ME, a beautiful journey of accepting and loving myself so I can spread that love to others.

Chapter 2

THE NEED FOR SELF-CARE

One way to feel good about yourself is
to love yourself... to take care of yourself.

—Goldie Hawn

Stress is the modern epidemic and one of the biggest stressors we can face in life is divorce. If we don't take care of ourselves when tragedy hits, the stress can wreak havoc on our bodies physically, mentally and emotionally. It manifests as compulsive behavior and self-destructive habit patterns that when not dealt with destroy our family life, work life, and social life.

Most of our cognitive functions occur in the brain but our cells also speak to us through "molecules of emotions" that are found throughout our body. Your brain and each cell of your body depend on the functions of all organs of your body to provide the energy, oxygen, and means to detoxify each cell as the body's metabolism processing molecules. Put in simple terms, your digestive tract, circulatory system, liver, kidneys, and almost every organ system of the body are involved in supporting the higher functions of your brain.

You can't fully escape the outer stresses of the world until you work on the inner, harnessing emotions, detoxing from them and replacing them with new beautiful memories. So you must first take care of your mind and then treat your body with loving care. Pay attention to what you put in your body because balanced nutrition keeps your body functioning as it's supposed to and it supports your mind and emotions helping you to deal with stress.

You are responsible for your "temple" that you live in. You only get one body so it's imperative to take care of it. Your body is the playground of consciousness and energy, so to keep our energy flowing here are a few additional ways to combat stress: deep breathing, Tai Chi, Yoga, Meditation, guided imagery, and prayer.

The mind is the primary medium that creates stress. Yogis have known for thousands of years that the mind is the fundamental cause of physical, mental, and emotional suffering, that's why they use meditation to disengage from their thoughts, feelings, and emotions that arise from the toxic body as well as remove the toxins from the body.

Many people are not comfortable sitting in silence with their own mind but the more you try it, the more comfortable you will become and the quicker you will heal. Life is a playground full of beauty and magic, it's all up to us if we choose to see and experience it that way. We were not born to suffer!

Letting Go

Divorce Can Be Shocking

There is such a flood of emotions that spawn after divorce and one of the biggest ones is shame. What is wrong with me? Where did I go wrong? How could I have prevented the divorce from happening? Why didn't he love me? Why am I not good enough?

If you find yourself in this twister of emotions, it's time to pause, take a deep breath and silence your mind. Yes, take a time out! One of the best ways to get all of that garbage out of your mind is to write it down in a journal, even if it ends in ink vomit. Keeping those emotions inside will lead to more wreckage in your life as you attract a reflection of where you are.

I found myself doing just that after experiencing a painful divorce. Through my journaling, I was able to heal and realize that true love comes from within and the key to recovery is finding gratitude in the midst of the storm.

You can't write that. You can't tell that.

This is what went through my head right after I got off the phone with Dawn about doing this piece. And it embarrassed me. Why? Because I've been divorced for a good while now. Because I could have (and would have) sworn I was no longer held captive by these phrases. Well, I guess I was wrong about that, but…I'm writing about it anyway.

How It All Started

I want to say the common thread of my story is perfectionism. It started early. I'm the oldest of three children to extremely loving and open-minded parents, so it was just easiest to be good at everything and not ruin the sweet ride. It wasn't that I was afraid of punishment; I just didn't want to be punishable. I wanted to keep that twinkle I saw in Mom and Dad's eye when they said my name or looked at me. I wanted their approval and avoided their disappointment like the plague. Praise was intoxicating. And I was really good at being a perfect kid.

I got great grades, took all honors, and made every team or squad or ensemble I tried out for. I never got grounded or Saturday School (my high school's version of detention). I didn't drink until I was twenty-one. And I didn't say one curse word until I was nineteen, and even that was by accident. Don't get me wrong; I was far from actual perfection. But as far as I could control that, I did.

Of course, when you're consumed by being a perfect child, you don't learn how to fail very well. And so if perfection is the common thread here, I'd say that thread was cut on my nineteenth birthday.

I was born in Los Angeles in the 80s. My parents lived out

there for a little under a decade during Dad's rock guitar days. 80s rock calms me down to this day—especially electric guitar solos. In 1990, they moved back home to Nashville, and we've lived here ever since. Kindergarten through college as a Tennessean makes me a Southerner in my book, and the South is typically known as the Bible Belt. More specifically, we are the buckle of said Belt.

My house was not religious but rather spiritual. Actually, I take that back. My house was all about love. Loving your neighbors. Loving those who didn't think like you or look like you. Loving those who were struggling with addiction. You name it. My dad's job (and home recording studio) brought all kinds of folks into our world, and the only rule was to love them all. We didn't have to agree or follow suit, but we had to love them.

The home was different than school though. I went to Christian private schools where religion was part of the curriculum. On its face, that's not a bad idea, and I'm not here to dispute anything about it. However, it is important to my story to talk about the effect the pairing of religion and rules had on me. The biggest of these rules I'm talking about centered around morality, modesty, and sex. You either were a "good Christian girl" who wore clothes that were tasteful and did not engage in any sort of sexual activity or…you weren't.

Even with my pursuit of perfection, I seemed to straddle this line. I wasn't modest in the slightest, having grown up in a leotard for dance and gymnastics. And I had kissed boys and done other things, but no sex. No way. Not until marriage. The Bible said it was wrong, wrong, wrong. And that was that. I had no trouble not having sex before marriage. It wasn't up for discussion in my book. It was perfectionism personified; the only rule that really counted at the end of the day, in my opinion. So when I told my boyfriend during senior year of high school this, he said he understood, I believed him.

It was my nineteenth birthday when I lost my virginity in his dorm room. To spare you the details, I'll get right to the gray parts, the parts that plagued me for years: I didn't know what was happening until it already was happening. Yeah, I know. It sounds unbelievable. But one minute, I'm fooling around, the next I'm crying about something out of absolutely nowhere (I still don't know what I was crying about to this day), and then...I was in pain. At first, I had no idea why, and then it struck me what was happening, or more accurately, what had happened. I was frozen. I didn't say anything. I didn't participate. I just kept crying. And then it was over and I went to sleep a changed girl. Happy birthday to me!

You could ask why I didn't say anything or push him off me. You could say it was my fault for fooling around. You could ask why I stayed his girlfriend after that and why it took me over a month to build up the courage to say I didn't want to do that again. I asked myself all these questions. And because I thought it was all my fault, my answers weren't acceptable to me, so I told no one.

Perfection obliterated. And I didn't know what to do next. He broke up with me around midterms (a few months after my birthday), and I sank to a new level. Everyone just assumed it was the break up I was struggling with, and I let them think it. It was easier than starting a sentence with "I need to tell you something."

Post-Perfect

A silver lining here was that I did write my first song about it, and even more special, I co-wrote it with my dad. "Good For Goodbye" was a powerful song, but it was a lie because

I wasn't good with it at all. I wanted a do-over. I wanted a time machine to go back to that night and keep my clothes on. Or not travel up to see him that weekend. Or something! I wanted the old guy back. Not the one who had changed. Yes, I missed him. But I also missed the simple life I had before. Life before shame.

Shame consumed me even more than perfectionism, but I kept all of this a secret for years. I let it drive me to be perfect in every other way possible, almost to prove to myself that I was still lovable in God's eyes (and so in my parents'). Like I said before, I did not drink until I was twenty-one. I strived and over-achieved like a beast, graduating in three and a half years from Belmont University with a degree in music business. I signed a pop record deal and toured with Jordin Sparks, New Kids On The Block, and Backstreet Boys. I was on Ellen. I recorded two albums and filmed multiple music videos. I was living "the life" on paper. But I was just running from shame.

The Marrying Kind

Another thing that is prevalent in the South is getting married and starting a family fairly young. I adhered to it big time. My parents got married at twenty/twenty-one, had me three years later, and they've been happily married ever since. I wanted whatever they had—I still do. So, when I met my future husband, I thought everything was finally going to be OK in my world. Our first date was in 2010, while I was in between tours and right after a tumultuous break up with a guy I had actually broken up with multiple times. (I don't want to use my ex's name so I'll call him H for Husband.) H was a breath of fresh air on the heels of such a rocky relationship. He confessed a crush he'd had on me since middle school. He was enthused by my being a pop star rather than the negative responses I had gotten from other guys in the past who weren't interested in my rapid schedule changes. And he wanted to move to Los Angeles with me…in like a month. All things were a go. (At least, I thought so.)

We got married in September 2012 in Nashville. We were divorced in June 2016.

Between 2010 and 2016, there were signs. But two things were driving the car for me: 1. I wanted to be married because it meant I wasn't damaged goods after all. 2. I had grace coming out of my ears.

Let me explain the second one a little more. My dad is one of a kind. He still talks about my mom like they're dating. He loves that woman so much it's borderline sickening. Of course, my mother is more than deserving of every ounce of adoration she receives as she, too, is one of a kind. As a daughter, this common exchange was something to behold. And I wasn't the only one who noticed. All my life, I've heard my mom's friends say "they don't make 'em like your dad." These are compliments I realize, but I also started believing them as a truth. I subconsciously figured my dad was a sort of anomaly that I would have to lower my standards a little in order to get married before I was thirty. And that fact was evident in all my relationships.

So yes, there were red flags. They started out small, though, and gradually got worse as time crept on. H had a less than fun upbringing. His family was wrought with the drama that has yet to be resolved even now. At the beginning of us, he seemed to be turning away from that style of living. Come to think of it, no wonder he was willing to move across the country at the drop of a hat. He was running, too. While we lived away and I was on tour, I saw him very little. We would either be running around West Hollywood or Santa Monica in between rehearsals, studio days, or photo shoots trying to find some semblance of a relationship. It was easy when the time was finite and you were in a place like LA. Everything was a movie scene in itself. Plus, little time equaled little time to really get into super deep conversations.

By the time I stopped touring and we moved back to Nashville (much to his dismay), he could no longer stay away from his family or their impact on him. And neither could I. But even more than his family being a physical part of his daily world again, I honestly believed my career change (aka not being an artist anymore) affected how he saw me. I was an ordinary girl all of a sudden. No more tours or rhinestoned leotards. No more prospect of being the next Katy Perry. No more west coast lifestyle. I gave it up, and I think he resented me for it.

The red flags became more visible. I saw them in how H would talk to me, how he would talk about other people, especially his own family. And mine? Don't get me started. He had a lot of anger and bitterness toward anyone who had wronged him, and he set out to show them their mistake in doing so. He valued status and money. And he despised my open-ness about pretty much everything. Another red flag I tried not to see was our intimacy or lack thereof. I just didn't want to have sex. I assumed it was residual from my first sexual experience, so I vowed to go see all the specialists and read all the books and pray to God like it was my job to desire my own husband.

We got married anyway. Looking back, it was as if I believed at that time that marrying was the secret sauce, the finale that would end all my problems—as well as our problems—and put me right in the eyes of God again. Have you ever done something hoping it would fix everything? Spoiler alert: it did no such thing.

The Beginning of the End

In all honesty, I think the wheels started falling off right after we got married. But there were plenty of other things I attributed our tension to at the time. We had a lot going on. Since moving back from California, we helped his family business expand (and which I became a bookkeeper—yikes), went to real estate school, I was still a staff songwriter at the time for BMG, and I was writing a novel. Plus, we were newlyweds! The first year of marriage was no joke, and meshing our families seemed to be the biggest joke. I already knew we came from different backgrounds, but the divide got even bigger when we started our lives as husband and wife.

The first year was hard, but I thought it would be. I stayed and didn't think much of it beyond the fact that it wasn't as fun as I'd hoped. Year two would be better. Or maybe year three. Our hard work would eventually pay off, and we would have more time with each other. His stress would lessen. But, then we decided to move out of a small condo into a bigger house, expanded the family business even more, and he worked on a startup while I continued to write and sell houses. We never ever slowed down.

H's startup was in tech, so we made the decision to live in Santa Monica half of the year. He was all about it, and I still felt guilty about making him leave in the first place. His stress level always seemed to calm down by the static sunny weather and awayness of California, and Lord knew I needed him to be happy. I was still struggling with my lack of interest in having sex, and boy oh boy was it taking a toll on both of us. He felt neglected and thus angry at me, and I felt ashamed that getting married hadn't fixed me.

He started making comments I wasn't used to. I knew he wished my chest was naturally bigger, but the idea of surgery was now very much on the table. I didn't want to. If you see my body, you'll understand. I just don't have the real estate for it. It wouldn't look right at all. I told him this was how God made me. His response confused me. He said God made him like bigger chests. He couldn't change. But I could with surgery. Like I said, I was confused. Not appalled. Not indignant. I should have been (and I am now!), but during that time, the shame of not being what he wanted in a wife was just too much. I actually considered getting surgery because of it. I just wanted to make him happy for once.

Apparently, I didn't dress right. I wasn't put together or "adult" enough in my choices during the day, and I wasn't hot enough when we went to a function. One of the more memorable nights near the end of our marriage was the night of his ten-year high school reunion. The key here is to realize we went to the same small high school. I knew everyone in his class, and we regularly saw half of them at the restaurants and old football games. My point is that this was not the kind of reunion where you show up and impress everyone with all your crazy news. We all saw each other all the time. So, imagine my surprise when he questioned what I was wearing. It was August, so I had chosen a short skater skirt with a black top. It was cute, but it wasn't slutty. He said it needed to be tighter. I asked why. He asked how he was going to show everyone what he got if I wore that. You read that right. What he got as if I was going to be this big surprise to everyone? Did you marry Ashlyne Huff? Way to go, man! But, again, instead of anger, I tried on a few more options only to be told no. It wasn't short enough. Didn't show enough of this or that. And finally, he said he didn't care what I wore. Color me defeated.

These kinds of conversations were happening a lot. They all had an underlying theme: sex. I was so low about my abilities in the bedroom that I believed him on a base level. I knew how he talked to me wasn't right. My dad would never have said anything of the sort to my mom. But I was so shamed by my own past and present difficulties that I didn't fight what I felt like he was really saying: you're still not fixed. And it's ruining our marriage. So, it's on you, Ashlyne.

I want to sit here and write that I ended the marriage. That I got fed up with everything and just called it quits. That after attending marital counseling and seeing absolutely no change I would have known it was over. But he was the one. I made him say it, he was the one.

It was early March when he went back out to Santa Monica for a week or so. Before he left, we had had a huge fight (the last fight) that had rendered me unable to move the next morning. Not physically, but emotionally. It was my first time to experience debilitating depression. So, I told him we needed to simulate separation while he went to the west coast. No talking. If he wanted to call me, it needed to be to say two sentences: I can't live without you. I want to make our marriage work.

He called within two days, but it wasn't about our marriage. It was about an airport story. I was sad and pissed he wasn't taking it seriously. My dad was too, and he tried to help. On March 3, 2016, I was at my parents' house. I knew Dad and H were on the phone, but it had been a while, so I went to ask how it went. Right at the bottom of the stairs, I overheard my dad say "you need to tell her sooner than later" before he appeared at the top. We locked eyes, and the pain between us was startling. He knew I just found out I was getting a divorce. But the sucker punch angered me. I spun on my heel and went to get my cell phone. I called H, and in a measured voice, I told him I was going to ask him a direct question and he was going to give me a direct answer. Was he done fighting for our marriage? He said yes.

That was that. I was getting a divorce. And you know what? I was relieved. My family and friends commented on my lightness about the whole thing. For me, it was an answer. I knew I had done everything in my power to save the marriage, so I had no regrets. I also knew he had called the divorce, so he couldn't turn that back on me. I thought life was going to start getting simpler. Not so fast. It was three weeks later I found out he had been on Tinder for a year and a half. It was a crazy night by all accounts, but it did do one huge thing: finding out he had been cheating took me off the hook of shame about sex. No wonder I didn't feel comfortable undressing and being vulnerable. I strongly believe you know when something's off. I was just so consumed by my past that I didn't realize it was him that was off. Our bedroom wasn't a safe place, and my body knew it. Finding out about the cheating was the biggest gift. It made all the comments, all the body talk, all the anger in his voice make sense.

We were divorced by mid-June 2016. It wasn't fun at all, but it was pretty quick in terms of the legal process. Over-achievement came in handy here.

The Beginning of a New Beginning

I thought the day I got divorced would be the start of a whole new life. I was right, but I was also wrong. I assumed the whole new life thing would be more fun without the guy who seemed to dislike everything about me. I didn't see the intense loneliness or the self-doubt coming.

That first year post-divorce was way harder for me than the marriage or the divorce combined. I was crippled by everything: anxiety that I would never be successful, that I couldn't make it on my own, that no one would ever love me again, and that I was old.

My thirty-first birthday was all gloom and doom. My poor parents watched me stare at the wall with a limp face until my dad decided it was time for me to get a new dog. I didn't mention this before, but my little Yorkie of twelve years passed away in the middle of the night four days before mediation. Charlie had been my constant since I was eighteen. He was the first one I told about my sexual trauma, and we'd bonded because of it. He had heart disease though, and I had to take him to be put down when he stopped breathing. It killed me. So, on my birthday, my dad suggested we go to a shelter and find a new puppy.

Enter Ollie, my rescue. My little light. He was just sitting there in the crate with a cone around his head, scared and sad. I knew he was mine right when I walked in. And we've been inseparable ever since. He's weird and all wrong in so many ways, but I swear he has Charlie's soul. And he loves me unconditionally, which is so crucial after a big life change like divorce. I took him home, but he rescued me a hundred times over.

Unfortunately, just getting a new dog did not fix my self-worth and self-doubt issues. I didn't believe I could do anything anymore without the help of someone seasoned, so I went back to real estate and started working for another agent—years after getting my license. It wasn't a great fit from the start, but at the time, I was still somehow convinced it was me who was the problem. I stayed for about five months total until it hit me that I was signing up for a life I didn't want. I didn't get divorced only to feel like this!

In March 2017 (a year later from the biggest month of my life), I started making big changes. I went out on my own in real estate, which scared me to death. Real estate is the opposite of security, and security was what I desperately wanted to feel. I got a mentor, Carolyn, who is just the best ever. She was divorced when she started in real estate over thirty years ago, so she took me under her wing and encouraged me to set a goal for myself. This goal scared the poo out of me because I was sure I wasn't going to meet it, which would mean I failed again. Not perfect. Not good enough. All the things. But she said it was crucial I set it. I surpassed the goal, by the way.

But real estate doesn't make me tick. I love to solve problems, I love people and finding them a new place to call home, and I weirdly love paperwork, but real estate is not and will never be creative. And I need that in my life. So I found a way. It started with making closing gifts for my clients. I would hand-sew a tea towel with a funny saying for my clients' new kitchens. And then someone asked me to make five of the same one. Shoot. I did them free-hand. I couldn't reproduce! My mom was the first to suggest I figure out how to get my designs digitized so I could use a machine. Talk about a problem solver.

So, I did. And then I started designing. And then I learned how to hand-dye fabric. And then I added aprons. And then tote bags. And then my friend Keatyn (also divorced) came on board. Within six months, The Piecemeal Shoppe (piecemealshoppe.com) was officially launched. Piecemeal means "as you go." And there is literally no other way to live, is there? Especially post-divorce. I love making my pieces with my hands, making something beautiful, and making something that will make someone laugh or, at the very least, crack a smile. And this may be petty, but I'm thrilled my ex-husband had nothing to do with it. This is my creation through and through.

As you've noticed throughout this chapter, I like to do

a lot of things. I have always been entrepreneurial, but this year of rediscovery has put that into overdrive. On top of real estate and The Piecemeal Shoppe, I started writing a book about recovery from something like divorce, and I got my yoga-teaching license. Yoga has been central to my healing process, so I thought why not learn how to share that healing? I realize I'm insane. But you know what? When in my life will I get a chance to do all of this all at once? One day, I will find someone. One day I will become a mother. One day, I will be comfortable living alone again and stop sleeping over at my parents' house more nights than not. One day, this part of my life will be a memory. And I intend on making it a fond one.

While I was doing all of this stuff, I performed a sort of self-autopsy on my life. Intent on not getting back to this place of intense depression and anxiety (I have the kind of panic attacks that make me sick to my stomach) ever again, I examined every bit of myself. Nothing was off limits, nothing is taken for granted. I had to know everything if I was going to change the course of my future. Like I said, I wrote about it not only in my journal (I've been journaling since ninth grade) but also in a memoir-style story of the hardest year of my life. I went through past relationships and found similar responses to the same old stuff. I looked at how my religion had played a part. I looked at how I saw myself. I started therapy again for a while, but ultimately I found the biggest emotional shift after I started seeing a chiropractor, Dr. Carlee Brockman. Her approach to pulling some of the yuck out of my physical body has been a game changer. It's like counseling and adjustments rolled into one.

My self-autopsy continues to this day. But what I've learned so far is this:

- Perfectionism isn't who I am. It's something I picked up to control my world. And if I picked it up, I can put it down.

- I might be a storyteller, a writer by nature, but writing the end of my own story before it happens only leads to disappointment. Instead, I write the word "curious" on my arm every day in Sharpie to remind myself of the kind of life I want to live. I'm still contemplating a tattoo, but until I decide...Sharpie. You can't be curious and write the end of your own story. It just doesn't work that way.

- I am not the product of my sexual experience. I am not a broken toy. I am lovable and the right man will not only see that he will cherish it.

- I am not a divorcee. I had a divorce. But it doesn't define me or have to be attached to my name like "Bestselling Author" or "Oscar Winner" in my byline unless I choose to attach it, which I don't.

- I am Ashlyne Anderson Huff. I am worthy. I am enough.

Instead of lamenting what I don't have, I have to decide to get what I can. Some things can't be forced, right? Like finding love, for instance. Or starting a family the way I want to. So until those come naturally, I am getting back to loving me. Being proud of who I am. And amazingly, I think I'm kind of awesome.

Now you may be wondering, where is Ashlyne today?

Ashlyne Huff is an author, songwriter, singer, dancer, yoga teacher, creator, and real estate agent—sometimes all in a twenty-four hour period. She's exhausted most of the time, but that's when she feels the most alive. Ashlyne grew up in the music industry and pursued her own musical path once she graduated from Nashville's Belmont University with a BBA in Music Business. With a pop record deal in LA, she was lucky enough to tour with the New Kids on the Block and Backstreet Boys, Jordin Sparks, appear on the Ellen Degeneres show and record two albums. After a three-year stint on the road, Ashlyne decided moving back to Nashville was best. There, she wrote a novel called *Falling Stars* about some of her experiences, started PiecemealShoppe.com, became a yoga instructor, and got into real estate. She currently lives in Nashville with her odd dog, Ollie.

Reflection

By now you are probably seeing a common thread between Ashlyne's story and mine. We both were survivors of sexual abuse but despite surviving, we weren't thriving when we met our spouses. This leads to a lot of destruction and added self-doubt, lack of belief in ourselves, shame, guilt, and a distorted perception of our true beauty.

Ashlyne is using a method of visualization, with one word, curious, as a way of keeping her focused and on track. The power of positive thinking and the realization that one day she will have all that her heart desires because in perfect timing the right man will find her as divorce does not define her.

Abuse can lock us in fear if we are not careful. There is a key step that Ashlyne took to catapult her on her healing journey and that was a self-autopsy, looking within to see where she was lacking most instead of numbing her pain and discomfort of past experiences. Looking within can be very uncomfortable but the best way to get on the other side of fear is to face it. Shame could have kept her bound but instead, Ashlyne gained the courage to reveal her secrets of the past and by doing so she is releasing herself from repeating her pattern, an opportunity to find true love from within, building up her self-worth so that the right loving partner can find her.

Chapter 3

GAINING CLARITY IN COMMUNICATION

The characteristics of an authentically empowered
personality are humbleness, clarity, forgiveness, and love.

—Gary Zukav

Communications is essential for a relationship to thrive and this includes untold words. It's estimated that 65% of marriages that end in divorce are due to communication problems. Due to traumatic experiences of the past, we hold back from being our authentic selves, causing communication to be distorted and in some cases non-existent.

Many of us have grown up looking through distorted love lenses and it's no wonder communication is the biggest cause of divorce. We communicate in the manner in which we have been raised, for example, if we grew up in an abusive home we have been taught that it's best safe to keep our feelings to ourselves.

Although you have every right to feel the way you are currently feeling from your divorce you don't have the right to impose it on others. So it's time to check in with yourself, take inventory of your feelings and how you are communicating those feelings to people around you. Realize that all the negative emotions you may be feeling right now, anger, jealousy, resentment, and hatred are due to you wanting something different from the person you married then what you received, and as painful as that may be to realize, it's important to understand that they came into your life to teach you something about yourself and to catapult you further ahead on your journey so that you can become the authentic amazing diamond self person that you were created to be. So grab your pen and start journaling, it's time to have a conversation with your thoughts.

Clear communication is possible if delivered through love. Relationships with others help us to reflect and realize the relationship we have with ourselves. This is why it's important to take a pause when exiting a relationship if we don't then we carry the same baggage with us, unresolved inner conflict, and we attract a mirror image of that.

The best relationship is the one with self in a non-egotistical way, it makes you feel free and helps you love others will no attachments which is the true vehicle for internal fulfillment. Remember once you have worked on yourself and you are healed, a whole person instead of a half, then the most loving relationship that will find you is one that enhances your ability to achieve your highest internal freedom to be yourself.

A Break in Patterns

The Story

What else do you do growing up in a small town? You guessed it. I was a cheerleader throughout my junior and high school years and was a "gifted and talented" student—as they called our batch of students—in those days. I worked a full-time job, outside of high school, and went on adventures with my best friend, when I wasn't working or with my boyfriend. Whatever I chose to do, I chose to do it at 100%.

This high drive was hard to manage when I was so young. "So young" —even to write that brings a chuckle, because I can remember, vividly, thinking I was "all grown up" when I was 17 years old. As my junior year of high school was unfolding, I found myself burning out. The class work was easy, and I didn't see the value in going to class every day. As soon as the football season and cheerleading competition were passed, I decided to fast-track the rest of my high school classes. I switched school districts so that I could take correspondence courses, in tandem with my classes, and I could double-down and wrap up high school. In those last three months of my junior year, I completed my junior credits, as well as my senior credits, needed to graduate. Once summer was over I had officially completed all requirements to receive my high school diploma. I walked away from being in the top 3 of my class, which I had been nearly my entire upbringing but now I had to decide what I wanted to do with my life.

After attending a College Fair, earlier in the year, the recruiters were calling. I had decided when I went away to whatever University I chose; I was going to go by my middle name. I wanted to leave "Tanya" in that small town. It was my chance to "be" who I saw myself to be. As the calls rang, and my Mom answered the phone, when they asked if Julia was home, it drove her nuts. Loving me, though, she would support whatever I decided. What I had decided, at that time, as I needed to get out of our small town so I could transform.

As I was making these plans to move off to College and evolve, a letter came that changed my course. Remember the boyfriend I mentioned earlier? Well, he was in the Marine Corp and had been gone about a year. We had broken up well before he decided to join the military, and honestly, we hadn't spoken in some time. That letter took me back to how I felt when we first started dating.

Richard was on the football and baseball teams in High School. Given the different seasons for the sports, he was able to play both—and he was really good at both. I first saw him playing baseball. He was a sophomore, and I was in eighth grade. The team was playing at home, and I ended up there with a girlfriend and her cousin, who was in High School. Not a baseball fan, I sat in the bleachers, in and out of thought. As the sun was setting, this beautiful guy was walking up to bat.

Wow! My full attention was on him. As the pitcher threw the ball, it seemed in slow motion as I watched this batter swing. He hit the ball and began to run the bases. I turned to Jessica to ask who that was—Richard. I was awestruck. Having an older brother that was a junior, I thought I was pretty familiar with all the "guys" in High School. I had never seen, or heard, of Richard. Now that I had, he was in the white space of my thoughts all the time. One Saturday morning, I woke up and went to the kitchen to grab a bowl of cereal. In my living room was Richard. What? How was he here? Why? As my brother, Eric, came into the room, he didn't introduce us, and I was glad. I was standing in the kitchen in my pajamas, hair a mess, glasses on, and in no shape to meet the very guy that I couldn't get off my mind! After his friends left, I asked Eric, "Who was that?" He said that was Richard (though he had no idea that I had seen Richard before, or had multiplying thoughts of him). I said, "Cool", or something of the sort, and went on with my day. My thoughts raced to be prepared to wake up every weekend morning, would Richard potentially be there? I couldn't meet him looking the way I looked first thing in the mornings.

As the school year ended, and I was preparing to enter High School, Eric hadn't had Richard over again. I had told my girlfriends about him, and how I was struck when I saw him. That summer, he remained in my daydreams. That is, until one night my phone was ringing, and when I answered it, it was HIM calling. How did that happen? Well, you have to love girlfriends that seize an opportunity. This one, I owed a big kiss to Misty for.

That night he called; we stayed on the phone for hours. When we actually met, the butterflies I was feeling were just as strong as the ones I felt from the first time I had seen him play baseball. As I entered my freshmen year, I was Richard's girl-friend. Life was great! Our friends all got along, and I couldn't be happier. The first year passed, then the second. As that second year began to wrap, we broke up. My heart was crushed. He had made some choices I couldn't support, and that was that. I ended up dating other people throughout the next year or so. I never stopped loving Richard, though. Your first love can be the hardest to let go.

The letter that arrived, years later changed my life. As I opened it, he was apologizing for any pain he had caused me. He said, "You are all I have thought about through Boot Camp. I love you." Pages into the letter, I was sitting in my bedroom, tears running down my face. I loved him. Even not seeing each other for years, how I felt in that moment was how I felt the many years before—awestruck with him. I wiped the tears away, finished the letter, and then began to write him back. I mailed my letter the next morning, and about a week later, the phone rang. This time, the person calling was asking for Tanya, it was Richard.

He was abroad for his current duty, and he had received my letter. As we spoke, we committed ourselves to each other, again, and began to plan when we would see each other. I caught him up on my University choices, and he shared with me the duty stations he had to choose from, once he was done with his serving on the ship. As we compared timelines, once he was stateside, we wouldn't see each other for about another year and a half. I was crushed! As we got off the phone, I sat happy—and sad—in the same moments. There had to be a different way.

We continued to write to one another constantly. He didn't have easy access to a phone, and phone calls were very expen-sive. The next time he did call, he had a plan of how we would see each other sooner, and every day, from that day forward. He proposed. Without hesitation, I said yes. He would be home within the next year, and we would get married when he was back.

As elated as I was, my Mom was the polar opposite. She gave me every reason why I didn't need to do this: too young, my future, College, it won't last, I deserved better (her opinion of pretty much every man in my life, from that time until I was nearly 40 years old). When I told her I was going to marry him, and I wanted her blessing, but even if I didn't have it—I was going to do it—she begrudgingly helped plan the wedding and reception.

On February 19, 1994, Richard and I were married in my hometown church. That very next day we were packed and driving to Jacksonville, North Carolina for him to report for duty. Within less than 72 hours, I had gotten married, moved over 1,000 miles away from home, and had no idea what I was going to do with my future (outside of being married). I remember sitting in our apartment, while he was at work, and just crying. All the future I had been planning, before taking a sharp left turn to marry my first love, was irrelevant now. In North Carolina, my Texas-based scholarships were also irrelevant, and we didn't have the means to pay for my education (student loans were not something I wanted to take on). I needed to determine a new path, now, and forge forward.

We only had one car; so working would have to be within walking distance of our apartment. I took a job at a small grocery store, overseeing the dairy section and running a cash register. Easy work, and something I had done in High School briefly. On my days off from the store, I would drive Richard to work, so I would have the car to run errands and such. On one of these days, I was paying our bill at the furniture store.

The manager stops by the counter and tells me he wants me to work for him. "Doing what?" I said. He responded with he wanted me to sell for him. He shared a few of the bullet points: pay, commission, and schedule. Clearly, I was going to have to think about this and talk with my husband.

The thought of being in sales excited me. The spark I felt was clear. Being a great salesperson was going to be my new goal. Richard was supportive but this means we would need a second car for this to work. We took care of that, and within a couple weeks, I officially began the professional journey into sales. Knowing nothing about selling, or furniture construction for that matter, I was ranked third in sales. With there being 10 salespeople on the floor, finishing in the top 3 your first month was unheard of. My second month, I took the top spot, and I held the #1 spot the rest of the time I worked there.

On the home front, Richard and I couldn't be happier. We had settled in our apartment, made friends to spend time with, and taken some short road trips. Neither of us had ever been to North Carolina, so driving up the coastline, and visiting the parks and such, was wonderful. We were a great team. That summer, he said he wanted us to have a baby. Oh, boy. He wanted to have a baby, but did I want to? I was just getting started in a career that excited me. What would happen to that if I were pregnant? I didn't want to lose my job. I knew I wanted to be a Mom, someday, but the timing seemed off. A couple of months later, we found out Richard was going to be stationed in Japan for six months. After a break-in scare at our apartment, we decided it was best that I go back to Texas for this deployment. I let my boss know I would be leaving and though he hated to hear it (no one wants to lose their top salesperson), he was understanding—and said there would always be a job for me, there, when I returned. Even though he was kind enough to say that we both knew I most likely wouldn't be back to Jacksonville. After a tour, a Marines' duty station seemed to always change.

Going back home for six months meant an abrupt break from building my new career. As I considered this, and the reality that these required moves could happen often, I revisited the thought of having a baby. The reason I had run from the idea was work-based. Constant moving was going to make that nearly impossible. A Mom could go anywhere in the World. That's it. We could have a baby, and I would make being a great Mom and wife my goal. Richard was elated. It was the fall, by this time, and we were only together for another month. We both knew it was unlikely I would become pregnant before his Japan duty.

The time came for me to be in Texas. Richard drove me, stayed a couple days, and then he was gone. I was back in my parents' house, with nothing to do for the next six months. Doing nothing was not a space I was comfortable in. My Mom knew this. She made a few calls, and within a couple days, I was working at Kim's, a local gas station. I also decided to take some college courses, since I was in our home state. I settled into both pretty quickly. A couple of weeks into my homestay, I felt odd. I was an avid Diet Pepsi drinker, and the Diet Pepsi wasn't tasting right. I chalked it up to a change in incredients. A month being home, I realized my menstrual cycle hadn't come. As I began to connect the dots, I bought some pregnancy tests. As I tested one, two, and three tests—all positive. In the small window of time, we had decided to start our family, I had become pregnant. When Richard called, I shared the news. To say he was excited is an understatement. He wanted constant updates on how I felt. As the months passed, and my body was changing, I would send him pictures. Those months flew by. At some point during all this, he told me we were being reassigned to Savannah, Georgia when he returned. I remember feeling sad about this because my small glimmer of hope to return to Jacksonville was gone.

The Move

We were settling into our new place in Savannah at the beginning of the summer. Being pregnant, and in the last trimester, during the summer in Savannah was dreadful. I had gained 70 pounds, and the heat and humidity made it unbearable to be outside. The depression I felt when we previously landed in Jacksonville was back. We had no friends or family here, and all I could do was sit in our 850 square foot apartment and watch television. When Richard got home, he did his best to console me. After a couple months of this routine, the time came. I was in labor. On August 12, 1995, our beautiful son was born at 6:37 p.m.

Jordan's birth gave me new challenges, and I have always loved a challenge. Until his birth, I had never even changed a diaper! You can imagine all the new life skills I learned as a new Mom. Once we were home and settled in, a routine was set pretty quickly. I enjoyed every moment with him—and being the first to catch his milestones. With all the joy that comes with being a parent, I found myself wanting for more—still. When Jordan was about 6 months old, we found a great care provider, Freida, to watch over him while I returned to work.

Furniture was the sector I was familiar with, and I was hired by the first place I applied. Within a few months, the manager wanted to promote me to Sales Manager. I quickly accepted. With added responsibility came more money, and more need for my time at work. Richard was supportive, at first, but what began to unfold was a conflict we hadn't been faced with before. He couldn't understand how I wasn't leaving work at 7 p.m., as the schedule reflected. His job afforded him that. It started and stopped, as he chose to do so. Dealing with customers, and their schedules, doesn't create the stop and go choice he knew.

I loved my job, and my new role and challenges, the more I loved it, the more I felt Richard resented it. In his eyes, the job took me away from our family. In my eyes, it was providing me an opportunity to better our family, financially, and establish a career I could help support Jordan with. The resentment Richard felt became the resentment I developed toward him. Our communication had all but stopped. Arguing with no resolution leads to continued conflict. One night, when I returned home late from work, he gave me a letter. The letter had the same words, and conflict, we were clearly not resolving. In hindsight, the letter was his attempt to communicate in a healthy way—as our arguments had usually escalated to his yelling. How I saw that letter, then, was the final straw that we were not going to be able to get on the same page—and the letter validated my feeling that we couldn't communicate. He was miserable. I was miserable. I didn't want Jordan to grow up observing parents that can't communicate, or even more, having to yell to try and prove a point. He deserved better. We all did.

Divorce

In a blink I was a single Mom—and still trying to build a career to support my son. We stayed in Savannah for about a year, but it was clear to me that I needed to get Jordan around extended family. I sold our house, and we returned to Texas. I took a break from career building, working a couple roles that were comfortable. I was home more, but I wasn't going to be able to provide any quality of life for Jordan, long-term, that way.

It seems like, only a moment after, I was back in full swing, professionally, and was having great, success. Within a couple years, I had been promoted to a Regional Supervisor, and Rose, my Regional Vice President, really needed me to move more centrally to my market. In June 2000, Jordan and I did just that and found ourselves in the Dallas/Fort Worth metroplex. A couple months after, he started Kindergarten, and I continued to try and balance it all. We were opening new jewelry stores, it seemed, nearly every weekend. Part of an opening is to have a Grand Opening—a call to action that encouraged people to stop in. We had hired a DJ for an opening, in another market, and I thought it was a great idea. I hired that same DJ to handle the Grand Opening of my base store in Dallas.

During the opening, there was something about this DJ, Steve that I couldn't take my attention from. He was magnetic. When there was a lull in business, I gravitated outside, where he was, and wanted to know more about him. That conversation lead, to many more conversations, and in 2002, we were wed. When we returned from our wedding/honeymoon, I resigned from my job, and two weeks later, was home with Steve and Jordan. Getting married didn't require me to quit. There had been some fundamental changes in the Culture of the Company and being able to step away for the wedding allowed me to see that clearly. I was blessed enough to have a husband that supported whatever I felt was best.

Moving into his house, with all his things and memories, was a bigger obstacle than I realized. When we had first started dating, he had made some choices that put trust in question.

The energy of our connection, when together, masked that I hadn't really moved past it—and trusting him continued to be an issue for me. Being in that house, and trying to live among his collection of memories, became too much. If we were going to make it, we needed to move. I started looking for houses—and landed on a new build-out a few miles South of where we lived. I gave the deposit, started the paperwork, and would need to talk to Steve.

Steve was taken aback by my buying a house. I told him how I felt within the walls we were in, and if we were to make it, we all needed to move to a space that I wasn't anxious in. We came up with a plan to rent the current house, and we all moved into the new house when it was complete. This new house, this space with no memories, was sacred to me. That was to be short-lived, though.

Steve worked night and day, building his business. He was wired like that, and it was one of the things I loved about him. He never gave me a hard time if I had to work late, either. The hiccup to his working the way he did, though, was the only way we could escape it was to travel. The time together was great, but we did have to come back to reality eventually.

His High School class reunion was coming up, and he wanted me to go with him. He grew up in Florida, so I figured we would fly in for the weekend. As the date grew nearer, he told me that they were needing someone to DJ, and he had volunteered to do it. What was a weekend flight to reminisce was going to be a road trip to take gear and such. Not to mention, that meant he wasn't really attending the Reunion, he was working it. That's how I saw it. No, thank you. I booked a trip to Disney with Jordan, instead, and he could stop by for a couple days, on his way to the Reunion.

Rocky Roads

It wasn't long after the trip and Reunion that memories I didn't want were in our home. He had reconnected with a friend, and he had invited her and her son to come to stay with us. When she arrived, it was clear to me she thought of Steve as more than a friend—whether he realized it or not. When I questioned him about her, he was adamant there was nothing there. As we sat at the kitchen table, one evening, she made a comment that completely dismissed that I was his wife. There had been small intentions she had made, up to this point, but this was the moment I broke. I needed to escape.

During a quick jaunt to East Texas to visit my parents, I was able to have the space to look at our relationship. Reflecting, I realized that trust had never really returned. I had masked it with a new home but I had now realized he had an unconscious habit of "white lies." The problem with this is I could never really tell if he was telling the truth, or not. He was raised to say what didn't cause pain, whenever you could. I was raised to be honest, regardless of the pain that might come. As I drove home that Sunday evening, clarity hit. Our values didn't align, and it was at the root of our issues.

Another Divorce

Steve and I tried to talk through it. We tried to go to counseling, over the years, but one of us having to change who we were—at our Core—was more than should be asked of someone. We both agreed it would be better to divorce. In November 2005, we did just that. Amicably, we rode to court together, and we hugged goodbye when it was over.

Married, and divorced twice, I was ashamed of myself. The example I wanted to set for Jordan wasn't going the way I wanted it to. When I married Steve, the desire to have a family nucleus—Mother, Father, and Son—was at the top of the list. Jordan deserved that. Inside I felt that I had failed. I was going to have to find other ways to be the example, for him, because I wasn't the least bit interested in ever getting married again.

Though I dated, and had some longer-term relationships, being Mom and Career Woman were my top priorities. As a woman, though, there are still emotional and physical desires. The seven years that followed were grueling, on this level. It seemed as soon as I would stop dating a certain type of guy, the next guy would turn out to be the same way. We are all familiar with the thought that there are givers and takers. As a giver, I was in way over my head with being taken advantage of. As 2010 came to a close, I began to wonder what it was about myself that I didn't value enough that I allowed myself to be treated this way. Professionally, I would never tolerate what I had in my personal life. Seeking the answer to that question leads me on a sacred journey of self-discovery.

The Analogy

How did I like my eggs? Julia Roberts, one of my favorite actresses, had played a character that ran away from the altar multiple times. No one could really figure out why. After the last time she did this, though, she went on a journey to discover why. What she found was that she became who the other person wanted her to be in every relationship. Richard Gere had been on a mission to write a story about her when he would ask the abandoned grooms how she liked eggs. Each said she liked them the same way they did, and each liked a different way of having their eggs prepared. It really made me think about what I wanted and what I was getting when I started a relationship. I needed more than to just give.

Patterns in Dating

Over the next year, I tackled the task of getting to know who I am—and to appreciate and value that. I had committed to myself to not be distracted by dating, so when the time came I was ready to venture back into it, I signed up for an online dating site. I met a few people, and I ended up dating one in particular. Within a few months, he had moved into my house, disrupted my son, and reminded me of the many others I had purged. What happened? Realizing this, I got him to leave, packed all his things, reclaimed my sacred space, and deactivated my online dating profile. Though I was frustrated I had attracted the same kind of person, as before, I had recognized it quickly—and responded accordingly. Not again.

Given I wasn't going to meet someone by intentionally looking, I decided not to look at all. I was good at this. My best friend, Jennifer, was not. She was constantly sending me pictures of guys and saying she was going to set me up. She would list all the reasons I should be interested—and I would graciously decline. Nearly every weekend I was at work, I would check my phone to find a new picture, of a new random man, being sent from Jennifer. It became comical. That is, it was comical until it wasn't anymore. It was the summer of 2012.

Jennifer and Kevin, her husband, had just left the gym and called to catch up. Jennifer couldn't wait to tell me about this guy she and Kevin had lined up for me to meet. No, thank you! She said this one was different. She sent me a few pictures, only later to find out she stole from his social media. Ok, he was attractive, but so what? Conversation continuing, she convinced me to meet him on Sunday, to watch the football game, with everyone.

The meeting was easy. I was attracted to him. He was a single dad, with a daughter a year older than Jordan, and he had three pets. I was a single mom, with Jordan, and three pets. He had two dogs and a cat, and I had two cats and a dog. I found that entertaining. By the fall of that year, Vince and I were dating each other exclusively. Jordan had met him, and he liked him. Jordan didn't like anyone I dated. Getting to know him, and myself, was a journey toward a better version of me. Vince was humble, and the least judging of others I had ever met. It was almost nauseating. His kindness was immeasurable. He would joke and call it "Catholic guilt," as to why he did so much for others, but it was clear it was a part of who he was. He was a giver.

During that first year of dating, Vince met my parents. Meeting my Mom, as you can imagine, was always an experience. She had nicknames for every husband/boyfriend of mine, she ever encountered. What would she nickname Vince? I would talk to my Mom every couple of days, so when I felt the time was right to ask, I cringed and asked her what her nickname for Vince was. She didn't have one. My parents had a running joke that no relationship made it longer than three years with me. She told me to ask her, again, after we had been dating for three years. As much as I hated to hear her say that, there was truth in that statement. Remember when I said I was raised to be honest? Now, you know who I got it from.

Three Times Is a Charm

One year turned into two, then three, then five. As time unfolded, Vince and I got to know each other even better than we know ourselves. We could answer each other's thoughts, and we knew when the other needed a little space to be silent. Conflict? We had a few big fights, over the years, and the missing link to every relationship before which was now resolved is that I finally learned to fully trust. In September 2017, the day before our dating anniversary of five years, Vince asked me to marry him. I said yes.

When the news was out that we were engaged, the calls came from my friends to razz me. I had told them, many times, I was never going to get married again—and I was good with that. On the other side of a hard time, every one of them acknowledged how special Vince and I are together. Some even commented on how, since being with Vince, I had become a better person. When you choose to be in a relationship with someone that has the same values as you and brings ones to light you didn't realize you were lacking, you are forged into a better version of yourself. You make each other better.

What about the nickname? My parents were in town the month after we were engaged. I was throwing a birthday party for Vince, and they drove up to celebrate. Sheri, Vince's Mom, in casual conversation asked my Mom what her nickname for Vince was. She said he wasn't going to get one. Mom had not only accepted Vince. She recognized that he was the other half of my whole.

Look Where Tanya is Today

Tanya's career has been focused around the success of those that trust her to lead them. She has developed hundreds of leaders, and thousands of team members, to drive results and operate at their best. The commitment she takes on spans beyond a job, and the overall retention she maintains is an anomaly in the jewelry industry. As an engagement ring expert, she has appeared on CBS, NBC, ABC, TX21, along with countless printed publications. With the ability and desire to support more people, Tanya spent years obtaining her education and accreditation as a business and life coach. Her tenacity to reach more people in their journey of growth and development lead to her starting her coaching, consulting, and speaking practice, Support Your Goals, she is the author of the book, Be YOU.

Reflection

There are so many amazing golden nuggets that you can take from Tanya's story but the first is communication. She recognized that communication wasn't matching up with the words that were coming out of these men's mouths and their actions. That's because body language is 55% percent of communication and words are only 7% so ladies watch for the signs. Once Tanya recognized there were lies being told she took action and removed herself from the relationship. The biggest healing measure she took after that was to turn within, recognizing that she was repeating patterns in attracting the same type of men and took a huge pause in dating.

Bravo to Tanya for recognizing that she got with her second husband because of a story she played in her mind, "to be a family." I have met so many women that jump from the frying pan to the fire because they want to have a father figure for their child and fill a lonely void for themselves in the process. If you feel yourself as a reader moving into this direction, take a pause and ask yourself is what you are about to do feeding your past or is it feeding your destiny? This is where there is power in silencing the chatter in your mind. Recognize that 95% of what we do on a daily basis is from the subconscious mind and considering that's our beliefs and past experiences it's important to look within, connect, and raise your level of consciousness which is where your true heart desires lie. I cannot stress enough the importance of taking time out. Just as Tanya did from her string of relationships that I don't like to refer to as not working rather as life lessons that caused her to turn within, found the true meaning of happiness, which resulted in meeting her fiancé, a man she never looked for.

So, if you are struggling with communication and are in need of some assistance here are ten steps to put you on the right track:

1. Put yourself in the other,' shoes, try to see things from behind their eyes.

2. Take a deep breath and open your heart accepting all possibilities and remember that often we hold our own opinions out of ego and fear.

3. Ask yourself, "Am I being sensitive toward the other person's feelings or am I just concerned with the way I feel?"

4. Take inventory of your own feelings is your heart closed or open?

5. Be aware of what you want, ask yourself, "What am I really hoping to achieve from this conversation?" Make sure your desire is not to change or control your partner rather for you to be heard and understood reaching a mutual compromise.

6. Meet the other person where they are at, if they are speaking in a low tone use a low tone. When we raise our voice it puts the other person on the defense.

7 Watch your thoughts, are they coming from a loving place or self-serving place? This can be hard especially when you are in a toxic environment but our goal is to always stay connected within, not lower to their vibrational level.

8. Be accurate and specific when you speak to the other person, supply facts instead of just emotions.

9. When speaking think positively of the other person. If your thoughts toward them are negative your words will reflect your thoughts as your mind is connected to your body. Remember tone is 38% of language, body language is 55%, and although words are currency they make up 7% of language, so when you speak make sure you are coming from a connected place with self so all is aligned with your intentions.

10. Say only what is necessary and don't waste time, this will only burn up unnecessary emotional expressions. Less is best!

Timing is everything, it's important to pick the right time and the right setting.

Just remember miscommunication is usually a clash between two people trying to guard themselves to remain secure.

Chapter 4

PUSHING PAST FEAR

I learned that courage was not the absence of fear, but the triumph over it. The brave man is not he who does not feel afraid, but he who conquers that fear.

—Nelson Mandela

Whatever we fear or struggle with on the inside eventually follows us. Our subconscious mind creates chaos for those around us when we don't harness what I refer to as the inner beast, our ego. We become attached in marriage to what we want life to look like and then when something goes wrong and the corner is turned, we tend to fall to pieces. This is why it's essential at all times including during marriage to work on our inner self and heal old wounds of the past or before you know it we are coming unglued. Life is a journey and healing doesn't happen overnight, it's a process.

Many times what we fear isn't real, we decide in our mind the worst possible scenario as an end result and then it becomes so gripping we believe it. I know firsthand, I stayed many years in an abusive toxic relationship, going through all the scenarios in my mind of what could go wrong to the point that I became trapped. It wasn't until I started studying mind-body connection that I made the shift and started looking at the possibilities of the life I could create. That's the key, meeting fear head on, changing your mindset and opening up to new possibilities understanding that there is a component of time that doesn't belong to us so we move forward bit by bit, step by step until one day we look back at all the magic that has happened in our life. I had to keep a gratitude journal because it gave me hope in the process of waiting and when you have hope, there is very little room for fear to creep in. Life can sometimes feel scary but it doesn't have to, if you just focus on showing up and taking everything one day at a time, finding gratitude in the little things which later attracts the big breakthroughs.

I am confident that you can push past your fear if you give yourself the time that you deserve and focus on your healing journey instead of finding someone or something to fill your void, which eventually will be fleeting. Focus on each day and release from the outcome and all is destined at the end of the day to be well in your world when you do your part.

Rebounding From Rock Bottom

When you've hit rock bottom, it can be easy to believe that there's no way out. It can be easy to stay stuck in the darkness grasping for your self-esteem and confidence. Going through a divorce was one of the most difficult things I've ever done as a man. Everyone talks about "single moms" in society, but what about single dads? I can assure you it's just as painful for us.

There are three significant lessons that I learned about overcoming adversity through a divorce.

Lesson #1: I learned about my own failures and weaknesses.

I learned that I was creating my own adversity to have to overcome by being resentful towards my ex-wife's role in our relationship as a stay at home mom after the twins had started school. I created a "whoa is me" internal attitude that I passive-aggressively took out on everyone around me especially her. It bled into my work and led to many self-created obstacles. Acknowledging and overcoming this adversity that I created has been a great lesson from my divorce. Sometimes the thing you have to overcome is your own imaginary creation.

Lesson #2: Kids can teach us how to navigate many things in life.

I learned another lesson on overcoming adversity through my divorce by watching my kids deal with the divorce, each of them in a different way. The adversity that they have had to overcome is a burden they never asked for or wanted but yet they persist. They trusted that their parents wouldn't make a bad decision about their family. They don't rebel or act out. Well one of them has but he's past that now and that's a completely separate story. If they can have that load dropped on them and persist with faith than I can overcome any adversity if I decide to.

Lesson #3: Things will always get better but they may get worse first.

When we had just broken up I could barely see past all of the emotionally driven conversations between us. I knew what I didn't want and I was willing to take many smaller losses to avoid the biggest loss with no guarantee that it would pay off. The amount of emotional adversity I had to overcome was a great teacher for handling my emotions in heavily emotional situations. It's like being a fighter in the ring in front of the cameras and being egged on by your emotionally charged opponent. Whether you're McGregor or Mayweather the fists are up and you're ready to go. Both parties come to the fight expecting a brawl. But what I learned is that you don't have to come in expecting the fight to be a battle. You can have grace and regain your character even if it actually is the biggest fight of your life. It's a fight to separate, grow, love, and reclaim your integrity and emotion. It's a fight over possessions and kids but the most alarming fight of all is your own peace of mind.

The lesson I learned in overcoming adversity here is that if you push through, knowing your outcome in your mind, that idea becomes reality. You've got to push through the fight and the adversity and remain committed to the not so pleasant path to get there. No one goes into a marriage desiring divorce. But sometimes it's just unavoidable. No pain, no gain. Sometimes you have to lose the dream you had and fight for a new one to grow. Sometimes the best thing for your marriage is to understand that you make better friends than partners. I learned that if you have a vision of how you want the relationship to be and you stay committed to that vision, even when you want to explode, when the dust settles, it's exactly what you pictured.

Our divorce was the most painful and beautiful lesson I have learned so far in life. Looking back, I can see where I should have zigged instead of zagged or stood up when I chose to sit but in the end, it's exactly the way that I pictured it. The unsaid was said and we both understood. We both grew as humans and our kids watched us handle it beautifully. I'm proud of us.

Eddie's Triumphant Position

Today, Eddie Martin is a 35-year-old divorced father of three who has spent the last 15 years as a top producing sales consultant and leader in a variety of blue and white collar industries. His primary focus is the continuing development of his mindset and sharing his discoveries with the world around him. After his divorce, he became more conscious of what his living legacy was and he continues to make every day a new opportunity to create and live his legacy to the fullest. Recently, he has been asked to speak on stages, lead training, write articles, and interview on podcasts. He believes these new opportunities are the by-product of his continuous effort to better the lives of those around him. Watching his children evolve into the world changers of the future is one of his most cherished blessings.

Reflection

Eddie faced his fears and worked through them and he also learned the power of mindset and how our thoughts become our reality. He could have chosen to let the fear of shattered dreams hold him back from growing and supplying comfort to his children but instead he stayed in the game, he took inventory of his thoughts and expressions of the past and gained courage to step up and correct his positioning helping him to supply a better environment for his children.

Spending time looking at our inner self is never easy nor comfortable but just like exercise, the more we do it, the easier it becomes. Everything about our healing journey comes down to choice, the decision to experience something different, a clearly defined desire and a solid plan of execution to make it all happen, the continual healing of the subconscious mind and the passion to want to win and make a difference. After all "It's not the load that breaks you down; it's the way you carry it." —Lou Holtz

Chapter 5

OPENING TO FORGIVENESS

It's one of the greatest gifts you can give yourself, to forgive. Forgive everybody.

—Maya Angelou

Holding on to anger and frustration only causes damage to us. Forgiveness is essential in relationships. Many people have the thought that if they forgive another they are releasing them from injury or insult. That's not the case, forgiveness is for self, choosing to release from judgment and shifting into compassion and acceptance. We can't have love and have un-forgiveness at the same time.

So many times our perceptions and thoughts are not accurate and we walk around with resentment in our heart towards others. When we choose to focus on the here and now, this present moment since it's all that we have, our perception changes. You can choose to be a victim or victorious. You can hold on to toxic thoughts which ultimately will create disease in your body or be victorious, send love, and understand that their suffering does not belong to you. Allow the other person to be who they are knowing that you can't control another person's thoughts or behaviors only yours. After all, why are you choosing to hold on to your fears and opinions? Do they define you? They should not!

Remember energy flows where attention goes and what has your attention has you.

When you free yourself from blaming others, it's then that you start living the life you really want. This involves releasing from judgment. It's ego that hangs on to unforgiveness.

When we don't forgive we are holding onto our own opinions.

Learning to love and forgive yourself, first supplies an openness for you to move on and be yourself. When we resist forgiveness we lock it in place. The process of forgiveness is simple, but not always easy, time helps heal. Sometimes problems are blessings in disguise. The best way to heal is through the use of higher consciousness. We can only create a better future when we release from our past.

Ask yourself, "Why am I holding on to my thoughts?"

I Am Enough

Do you have a memory of a message, either conveyed by actions or words, which plays out consistently throughout your childhood? Did it shape how you thought of yourself or some of the decisions you made as you grew up? Now that I am a grown woman, I think back on one I remember well, and it goes as far back as my memory will take me. I can remember, the message, it was "perfection!" I needed to be, do and pretend everything was "perfect," then I could get a man and live the "perfect" life; however, I had to be perfect to get him, and he had to be "perfect" too. He had to live up to an ideal she formulated in her mind, she who was never satisfied with anything, mainly herself which she projected on to me!

Past Defining Future

It was never verbally stated, just conveyed through statements meant to teach. "That woman is not married, wonder what is wrong with her." "You always put on lipstick before he comes home." "If dinner isn't ready, at least have onions cooking, so the house smells like it will be ready soon." "Wait until your father gets home" "Your father and I like your hair better short" "You are only pretty when you smile, you always need to smile." My personal favorite and the one that took me the longest to work through was from the night of my high school prom. I walked down the stairs, 5'10" with curled long blond hair, (straight is unacceptable), wearing a strapless, backless black satin dress with ballet flats, at that moment I measured 36, 24, 36. I wore natural makeup as we had spent the day in the sun out on the water. The first words my mother spoke to me were "You are going out looking like that?" Then you would see the infamous head lift and tilt, with a "hmmph," cementing her disdain and disapproval.

These and many other lines were ingrained in my head as I grew up, speaking the proper way to look and be so I could attain the ever elusive perfection that would enable me to get and keep a man. They were meant to teach me. But did they? Did I learn anything from this? Did they help me? Or Did they instill a belief in me that I am less than perfect? Not good enough as I was created. Since I am less than perfect, I can't get a perfect man. Living in these unrealistic expectations left me subconsciously looking for the first exit strategy I could find, and I found it.

Wedding Bells

He was in the military, a Ranger stationed in Fort Lewis, Washington, a "real" man .... or so I thought. I would later learn that it was a lie. The funny thing about learning something isn't true is that you don't always act on it. The first question I ask myself now is, why when I find out he had lied to me about his job, his identity, where he lives, did I not leave? Like most young girls, it was too late, and I had fallen in love with the persona of who I thought he was and who I would be with him, the ever supportive military wife — "perfect." About four months into our "courtship" he told me his unit was being transferred to Fort Polk, Louisiana. If we were to stay together, marriage was the only way we could afford it, and we agreed we would get married. Not only was it the only solution to us staying together, but it was my way out.

My mom hated him, and she would make disgusted noises whenever he would say something, or throw nasty looks, rolling her eyes as he spoke. We had brought crab legs home for dinner, her favorite, he cracked one open with his teeth, she threw down her crab and utensils, stormed off declaring she could not eat around such barbaric behavior. I am sure on some level I knew this would cost me dearly, but I had dug my heels in, this is what I was doing. Her behaviors were just giving me traction in my decision. Once I am committed to something, right or wrong, I move forward with 100% conviction. If I am wrong, I own that with 100% conviction too, but that didn't mean I was going to own it at that moment. At that moment, right or wrong, I was getting married. When your mother has made her disapproval known and that nothing has ever been "perfect" enough for her, why would one more thing make a difference?

In some weird way, I had manifested this guy and this marriage. There are defining moments in each of our lives where we want to be able to say we controlled something when everything else that we wanted stood just outside of our reach. At that point in my life, this was the ultimate "in your face" to my over controlling— nothing is ever good enough, perfection-seeking mom. He was the "bad boy image" "the Ranger" good looking and mysterious, and he was merely an image of what I thought could help me gain control. From the outside looking in, nothing of what I had ever dreamed of was in this package. It was my escape route, and despite it being the way out, I didn't know at this point what this was preparing me to navigate in the future.

From the lack of a proposal to the five-minute service in the Lakewood Chapel with none of my family present, no "reception" to celebrate, and the fight that followed that evening, we were starting off on the right foot, just "perfect!" He didn't even know why we celebrated Easter, so when I said I wanted to go to the Easter Service at the Catholic church up the hill from our house, his exact words were "why does everyone make a big deal about a goddamn bunny?" I was stunned, all I could think was, how do you not know about Jesus Christ? So began the journey of discovering his past, the darkness passed down to him, the little things that had happened when he was less than four years old, all of them shaping who he was today and, to him, a justification for the things he did.

Shortly after we were married we began the move to Fort Polk, we shipped what little belongings we had and then started the drive with the motorcycle loaded in the back of the truck. Some of my family was in California, they had offered to let us stay at their cabin in Yosemite for a couple of days, a honeymoon of sorts. We rode the motorcycle down to Sonora for some grocery shopping, and as I am packing up the backpack, I find three items, three costly things, I know we didn't pay for them. I was filled with anger and beyond furious to find out he stole them, and he could care less. As we made the ride back to Groveland, and we were winding our way up Hwy 120 and Old Priest Grade, I thought about what this road was known for; it's 18% grade and tight curves. All I had to do was let go, I would have fallen off the back of the bike, and that would be that. No more perfect expectations. No more unveiling the dark side of a husband who was nearly a stranger to me. Have you ever felt like that, that all you have to do is let go and find peace?

That was the first of many times I would feel that desperation for peace in the short two and a half year marriage.

Unfaithful

It happened one night again; I had come home early from work. He had been out at a bar when he came in; he had two bright pink lipstick kisses well placed on his chest. The pain I felt radiated through my body, I just could not comprehend how he let that happen, why would you do that? Why would you knowingly betray me? It wasn't right, and I wanted to SCREAM with the injustice of it all. He was incredulous; he could not understand why I was making such a big deal about it. "Who cares if some stripper kissed my shirt, that was as far as it went, why does it bother you so much? Don't you trust me? You knew I would come home to you." "Is that supposed to make me feel better, that it was as far as you let it go? A stripper? Am I not enough for you?" So went this dialog late into the evening, until I fell asleep from exhaustion.

The next day he wanted to show me how much he "valued" me, that I was important enough to him that he would spend money on me. Eric took me out the next day to "make up" for it, he wanted to buy me something from a jewelry store, oh YAY!! I went, saying no to everything he picked. Later that day, I found the two necklaces he had purchased with a "five finger discount" once again, there it was, that desperation.

One of my girlfriends from work had stayed over, he took

her home on the motorcycle, she wanted to ride it, and it was cheaper than my car. The radar detector read 120 mph as he outran two cops and traveled through two parishes, crossing onto the base and only stopping as he was faced down by an MP, a Military Policeman, pointing a 9 mm at his head. His foolishness proved to be a blessing, with the charges brought against him, I went to meet with his First Sergeant, the highest-ranking noncommissioned officer in charge of enlisted Soldiers. He agreed that if we paid the $1,200 in fines, he would discharge him, and I could get him back to Oregon.

Instabilities

It was a tumultuous year of breakups and reconciliations; he had lost job after job after job. Despite everything, I was blessed to be surrounded by a beautiful church community that kept me going and supported me. We were in the midst of dress rehearsals for a show I had choreographed for the church when the lights would hit, a wave of nausea would overtake me; I would run to the bathroom. Upon the fourth time of this happening, the director was furious, asking me to push through so they could tape one full performance. I did, and six months later my son was born.

Our New Addition

The realization that I now had a son made me ask a pivotal question? How do I leave now? How do I end things since there is a child involved? Thankfully, he was working for a seafood company and on a boat which meant he was gone for four months at a time. It was during one of these times that I was in San Diego for my brother's wedding, my son, Christopher was eight weeks old. My brother's phone rang, it was him, why was he calling, what was wrong? It seems that they were docking early and he would meet me back in Bend. The next day I called the company office to get the details of his flight and learned the truth—he was fired for sexually harassing one of his female co-workers. I was upset, but shock was not even part of my response anymore. No time for desperation now, my son needed a mom who was stable, I had a lot to figure out and choices to make about our future as a family.

He could not and would not hold a job. I spent my days working 10 –12 hours and taking my son with me to work four days of the week. I would come home to find he hadn't moved from the couch. Anger and frustration gripped me. I wanted to scream at him and demand him to tell me why he couldn't do anything while I was working so hard to support our little family? Wash dishes? Take care of the dogs? Vacuum? ANYTHING? Why can't you take care of Christopher during the day while I go to work? Despite that being a huge question for me, I would not have left Christopher. I didn't dare to leave my baby; this precious child that was entrusted to me with this person who thought hockey, day drinking, and accepting food from the church was acceptable living. This behavior was pathetic, but, as always, I worked harder to pick up the slack. My way of dealing with it was just to work harder, stuff your feelings where no one can see them, along with your emotions, and things will get better—Insanity, I now know!

What was it that kept me there, in this place of lying, stealing, secrecy, behaviors I had never entertained or tolerated in my life? What keeps you where you know you should not be, from moving forward to better your life? I needed to make it all right for him, to be there for him, to be the mother, nurturer he never had, that kept me there. My husband was the abandoned child, still stuck in that phase of his life, not being wanted by those who should have loved him and kept him close. I was not going to abandon him as he had already experienced by his father and his mother.

The sky was gray, the menacing clouds threatening to unleash the water they held, soaking him, as the harsh wind unwrapped what remained of the tattered bed sheet that had been around him. A baby, a little boy, sitting with his arms outstretched, screaming, crying out for someone, anyone, whoever had left him on this abandoned lot. That was the image that held me there, in this "relationship," that would never let me leave him—that was my bondage.

Until that night, the night when the bondage broke, that night, a simple request as I struggled to wake and cloth myself to stay warm while I nursed my son. "Please, can you hold him until I get up?" That night, the image of my son was stronger than any other could have been, the night I saw my infant son land at my feet, immediately replacing the picture I had held in my head for so long. I checked him; he was still breathing, his neck was stable, he smiled as I kissed him, I clung tightly to him as I grabbed my robe and left the room. It was time, no contemplation, no debate, the decision made.

The Decision

It was fast and furious, thankful for my dad's reputation and relationships with the police, I filed the restraining orders, hired the attorney, and moved into a new place. The next year had me sleeping with a pistol under my pillow, it stayed with Christopher and I as we moved nine times, with the ninth and final time taking us back to my parent's house after someone breached all the gates surrounding my house. Thankfully, we recovered my dogs unharmed, although they had a long stroll through the neighborhood, they were unharmed. The divorce process was taking longer than we all wanted; however, it was making progress.

It was a daily battle of fighting the perceptions of being a young, divorced mother; the anger for all that he had done that had chipped away at the people I loved the most, and it took all the control of my mind not to give the power to guilt for what I had let happen. I had broken my dad's heart, the man whose lap I could climb into and feel safe; the man who taught me how to work on cars, change my oil, change a tire and shoot a gun. The man that stood up for me, defending me saying it was my choice to do my school work or not, because he would not fight me on a daily basis and let it destroy our relationship. That same man who had always been there and no matter what loved me for me!

Self-Discovery

Throughout this part of my life, I learned a lot about myself. People would tell me I failed, and my response was and always will be that I did not fail, I learned what I didn't want in a relationship, I raised my standards. They say to make a list of exactly what you want; I didn't do that I made a list of exactly what I didn't want and went on a journey of rebuilding myself to attract the type of man that would be the best for both myself and, my precious child, Christopher. I had brought a beautiful, healthy boy into this world; he gave me a purpose to get up every day, and he gave me the reason to leave the situation I had put us in. Failure? No, I think not, God's plan playing out!

I spent hours in the gym working out, looking in the mirror, repeating out loud, "I am enough" over and over again, believing that if I said it enough, and acted as if it were true, I would feel it. I prayed every day that the Lord would show me, in no uncertain terms, which man was the right one for us. Countless times I cried outside my son's room, promising him I would find the best daddy for him. I am so very grateful my dad was a daily part of his life, guiding him, playing with him, taking him to Dairy Queen, that was a huge blessing and part of what brought me through to now.

During this time my mother had started showing signs of depression, I helped my dad take care of her and the day to day around their house. I had also begun working as a mortgage officer with a local company, Christopher was in a fabulous daycare, life was progressing. My focus was on establishing financial stability for my son and I, when I left, Eric stopped paying all the bills and was not paying any child support. I had tens of thousands of dollars in debt and creditors were calling daily, there was no real thought process around this other than to just get it done. I learned very quickly to not waste time in the thought process of how, why, when or what for, I just went about doing whatever it took to get it done.

My ex-brother and sister-in-law and I had thankfully remained and remain to this day, good friends, their Oregon home was not too far from my parents, and I was excited to see them as they were coming back from their home in Vermont. I had been the maid of honor in their wedding; our children were six months apart, we had a tight bond; they never knew how I ended up with Eric, but we all were thankful for our friendship. They were both Biathletes, a sport I knew nothing about other than they were very good at it, traveling the world to train and compete. The kids were excited to see each other, my sister-in-law Sonia, and I always enjoyed working out together, drinking coffee and just hanging out, we would take the kids to the club to play while we exercised.

Three people were running across the grass as Sonia, and I

stood to talk with her husband Rob outside the Athletic Club of Bend, the kids playing next to us. One of them stood out to me; I could see he had brown hair and a tank top on, and all I could think was hmmmmm, odd. "He runs weird," I said quietly, Sonia leaned over to whisper in my ear "that is what perfect form looks like, we all want it, and he has it." Good to know I thought, then all the runners I see must not know how to run. They got close enough for Rob to call out and motion for them to join us; he introduced me to his biathlete friends Curt, Debbie, and Dan. They all agreed to dinner at Deschutes Brewery that night, then proceeded in to do their perspective workouts. Sonia invited me to join; I declined, I wasn't looking to hang out and spend time "on the town." She persisted, telling that there was already a babysitter for the kids, it was to be fun, and her mom was there, she wanted to see me. Reluctantly I agreed.

Deschutes Brewery, as always, served up great food and drink, oddly enough, the only one to come out that night was Dan. So there we were—Rob, Sonia, Sonia's mom Louise, Dan, and I. We headed down to Cafe Paradiso for a coffee, then to other establishments to find some dancing. As the night wore on tensions became high, the energy pushing Dan and I together as it pushed our friends apart. We were on the sidewalk passing a parked GXSR 750, I stopped to look it to see if it was the same make and model as mine, "I have one of those" I heard Dan say, I turned and smiled "mine is a 650." I could see the mischief in his blue eyes "can I ride it?" he asked, "sure" I said, "if you fix it, you can ride it, there is an issue with the fuel switch." Thus began the first of many conversations between us, Dan did fix my bike, and we did ride it, less than a year later he flew back out, and he fixed the truck that Eric had wrecked. Eighteen months, one Olympics, many flights, and long distance calls passed, this man, this REAL man, asked my dad for mine and Christopher's hand in marriage.

New Beginnings

It was February 7, 1999, we were living in McCall, Idaho at 5,000 ft elevation, and the weather would go from sunshine to snow back to sunshine, with plenty of snow on the ground. Watching the clouds move out and the blue sky reveal itself, Dan grabbed my hand and said let's go. The kid next door came over to play with Christopher so Dan could take me out cross-country skiing. As we parked the truck I looked at the trail and thought to myself, are you kidding me, it was my eleventh time on ski's, and he wanted me to ski up that? He saw the look on my face, "Kellie, it will be worth it, the view at the top overlooks the whole valley, you have to see this." We headed off, I pushed hard and was thankful when we got to the top, he led me over to the outlook, he was right, it was breathtaking. We stood there silently admiring the view, it was magical, the lake, the mountains, this man by my side. He leaned over and kissed my head, I smiled and leaned my head into his shoulder. "I don't have money to buy you a ring, so I am giving you the one ring I do have and asking you to be my wife, will you marry me?" Tears streamed down my face as I took the Olympic ring he had earned and was now giving to me, "YES, yes I will!" As we stood there kissing, laughing, and hugging, the sky turned dark, as I looked out over the lake and said: "we need to go, that is a rain cloud." We had been there long enough that my ski's had formed a 3" ice ball on the bottom under my boot, I couldn't ski on them. We quickly traded ski's and headed down the hill, the rain pelted us all the way but I could not wipe the smile off my face as I "snow-plowed" Dan's racing ski's to the bottom, and he skied next to me on mine.

Our conversations have now spanned 21 years, missing only nine days during that time, multiple continents, one wedding, one adoption, a cross-continental move, two Olympics, one miscarriage, short hair, two more boys, building a home, starting five businesses, a deployment, multiple family members fights with cancer, long hair, the gaining and losing some of our beloved pets, one child heading off to the Marine Corps while the other two figure out who they are without him around, short hair again. The lessons I learned as I climbed my way out of that hole so long ago, unknowingly prepared me to turn my husband's deployment into a purpose to get up every day, to fight for, love and live with a passion; to make a difference, to leave an imprint, and create a legacy.

From April 4, 2005 to July 18, 2006, I navigated Dan's deployment while raising our three boys, 9, 3, and 2 and tried to maintain some resemblance of a "normal" life. At that time, I was working in the mortgage industry, homeschooling our eldest, studying equine psychology and behaviors, rehabilitating horses, building a hay barn, and developing our acreage. In 2009, Dan and I began Restoration Ranch LLC, our non-profit serving youth and adults having an emotional and mental diagnosis with Equine assisted Behavioral Coaching. As Dan advanced in his military career, we became increasingly aware of the level of disconnect the families had pre and post-deployment, and where our government was falling short, more often than not, our ranch and home became host to Soldiers as they came for their drill weekend. We became increasingly aware of the healing effects the horses, cattle and hard work of a ranch had on them.

Passion

Today, I write, speak, and coach to empower people through successfully taking their life's storms and turn them into their life's triumphs, with a special place in my heart for military families, parents, and kids. My goal is to help you find the answers that lie within you, recognize, define, and move into action on your life purpose. So now I ask you, yes you, the one who picked this book up because in some way it caught your attention, touched you or maybe just reassured you that you are not alone in this place. Now I say it is your turn! It is your turn to look at the hard part(s) of your life and be grateful for how it is a piece of the puzzle that makes you who you are today, celebrate what you learned and what you can do because of it. If you aren't quite sure how to do that, reach out to a trusted friend, or drop me an email, I would be honored to help you see the beauty in who you are.

Kellie's Success

Kellie Westover is a successful businesswoman, owning and running several multi-faceted businesses. She is a published author who has recorded the trials turned to triumph in her life and uses those stories to help others know that they too can be triumphant.

Kellie is a self-studied psychology and neuroscience geek; after suffering a Traumatic Brain Injury in her teens, she endeavored to learn as much as she could to help others that have experienced the same thing. After her husband's deployment, Kellie expanded her studies into Post Traumatic Stress Disorder, Pervasive Development Diagnosis, Autism and other diagnosis affecting children and adults today. She combined this with her Equine Psychology and Liberty Horse Behavior training and founded her non-profit Restoration

Ranch, a rehabilitation center for horses and humans. She has been contracted by schools and government entities to provide the equine-assisted behavioral coaching model she designed.

Wanting to expand her reach and certify her coaching, Kellie partnered with the John Maxwell Group and has become a highly sought-after expert in the field of coaching. She is passionate about helping you become your ultimate self, reclaiming a positive parenting dynamic, helping your teen successfully navigate today's world with their self-confidence and your sanity intact; or taking your relationship to the next level with the love of your life.

She enjoys working with military wives and families, millennials and their parents, spending time with her husband and three boys; she loves gardening, laying in the sun, fly fishing, writing, and spending time playing with her horses.

Reflection

We can't fully be in a relationship with another until we know ourselves and Kellie was brought up with the perception that she had to be perfect. That's what happens, we learn from our parents, we take those teachings out into the real world and try to find success and happiness. But often times, parents have conditioned thinking due to a generational belief system that is incorrect. Due to the pressures of life, Kellie jumped into a relationship that she knew at the time to be best and it was also an escape hatch from the pressures of her past.

Kellie got caught up in a co-dependency situation as many of us do; she took ownership for her husband's problems out of fear of not looking perfect, but those problems didn't belong to her but they did greatly affect her until she made a decision to break free. What Kellie did, took a lot of courage.

You may be going through a similar situation, but know that this too shall pass as tough as it may seem and with faith and focus you too can rise up from a victim situation and become victorious just as Kellie did. The most important decision of all is to not let fear hold you back to being a victim of bondage in an unhealthy environment. When we let go of what we don't want it's then that we can embrace life and experience what we do want. Everything we need to see is right in front of us that's why it's crucial to take time to yourself, go deep within, strip away the perceptions and all will be revealed, it's then that our healing journey begins. Learning to love self without limits!

Chapter 6

ATTITUDE OF GRATITUDE

The peace you seek lies in the kind stillness
between your heart and your spirit

—Kris Carr

One of the key expressions that turns around any situation in life is gratitude, the more thankful we are for where we are at, the more blessings and healings come our way.

Gratitude is one of the most effective ways of getting in touch with your soul. When you do this, you feel connected to everything in creation and you sense yourself as a force of infinite possibility. When you focus on all that which you are grateful for it opens you to the source of all the things that have come into your life. It also moves your EGO to the side because your gratitude comes from a loving place of consciousness from within. Keeping a gratitude journal listing, the things you are grateful for on a daily basis shifts your mind from expectations to the realization that you already have what you need. This draws you to the source of abundance.

The highest level of gratitude you can have is for the existence of self, knowing that it can be taken away in an instance.

Understanding that existence is a gift and not a promise. Thanking source for making you just as you are, another sign of self-acceptance operating from a place of the heart. You are stating that you are enough and you need nothing outside, you appreciate who and where you are at, at that moment in time.

When we operate from a place of gratitude a whole new dimension opens up, this is the dimension of grace. It's learning to live in a state of satisfaction all along the way for everything that turns up in our life, give it thanks. After all the secret to true happiness is being grateful for what you have right now, resulting in effortless joy, trusting, and knowing that all is well and what is meant to happen will happen and either way, YOU are OK; accepting oneself makes everything around you to become OK. But it's very important that your gratitude comes from an authentic place, your heart. Being grateful for whatever is showing up in life at any moment in time will squash all complaints and your life will begin to shift. You will no longer see issues or unresolved problems, you will just flow in gratitude allowing all problems to resolve themselves.

So start out by acknowledging the little blessings in your life, like your children and the fact that you are alive, a chance for a do-over. Make this a daily practice, after all, expressing gratitude is like having a knowing that all things show up in our lives for a far greater reason, usually to mold us, improve us and prepare us for something better. The higher the level of gratitude, the greater the supply of abundance, the more we transform.

"How often do you feel gratitude for everything you have instead of complaining about what you don't have?"

What are you grateful for? Is it material things, love and

connection with others, your body, your mind, understanding for self and everything around you? Whatever it is, get out a pen, start writing, and focus daily on the gratitude that brings love into your heart.

The Peace in Release

A Different Plan

"I could be a good wife…"

You ever get the feeling that something is over, but you just don't want to accept it? That is how I felt when I realized I had no reason to be married anymore. Divorce was something that never crossed my mind during that first 13 years. The concept that one day I might consider single motherhood over the traditional family unit wasn't something that could happen to me. When it all started to fall apart, I had all of the faith that God could heal my marriage. But he couldn't do it alone, and I certainly couldn't do it alone either.

Nearly 15 years of my life dedicated to one man, the one man that was charged to love, honor and cherish me all the days of our lives, was telling me daily that I was the worst wife ever. There were only two things that I wanted to be when I grew up: a mom and a great wife. I got both of my wishes, but it seemed I was failing at being either. I couldn't show my girls the loving home they deserved, and my husband told me every night that I didn't make him happy, and that I needed to do better. I believed him. I just didn't know how to make him happy.

At that time my husband didn't work anymore. He had taken off work on short-term disability for his back pain. Short term turned into long term, and to make a very long story short, here we were, nearly five years later with his severe prescription drug addiction and daily emotional abuse as our routine. At least I could see it now. The narcissistic abuse I had been going through since our first date was starting to come to light. It was like watching a bad movie you had seen before but without the rose colored glasses.

As my 30th birthday approached, I wondered what I could do to find a way to make all of this work. I didn't want the broken home that everyone in my family history had.

We had a planned summer vacation, and one day before our trip, he verbally attacked me in our hallway. I was used to being yelled at, but then he did something that stacked the deck against him. He brought our daughter into our argument. He used her as a weapon. He yelled at her and made her an example of what was wrong with me. My sweet little seven-year-old princess, playing in her room, not bothering anyone was now crying because she didn't understand what had just happened. I could take a lot of abuse, even knowingly.

But I would not let him attack my girls.

After our miserable vacation was over, I asked him to leave. "Give me six months without you here. We need a break from the fighting, the stress, and the tension. The girls need a break from it. Take the RV, go to the lake, and take a six-month vacation. I will bring the girls to you for visits and I can get some rest. We can come back to this marriage fresh and see if we can try again."

This was my compromise. My last try. If I didn't get a break I was done. I couldn't let him show our girls this example of marriage. The thought of them growing up and getting married, and choosing this life because "Mom did it this way." was unacceptable.

He refused.

My Marriage Analogy

At this moment I had a vision of every relationship resembling a cliff. You stand at the edge of the cliff, you and the person that you want to be with, and you wait. You wait for that moment when it's time to jump, and since there is only one parachute, in order for you not to die against the jagged rocks below, you both have to jump at the same time. If you jump, using all the faith you have that this is the right person when they are not, you may find yourself crashing very hard, very quickly, and very lonely at the bottom, despite wearing the parachute.

While this sounds dramatic, this is just a necessary part of any relationship and it is how we know who is all in, and who isn't.

This happened to me. The fall was immediate, the moment I said I do, and I jumped off that cliff. I was committed. The landing didn't happen for 14 years. What did happen was a slow hanging by a rope I didn't realize had been strung around my neck. There are moments in life where in order to live, we have to step out. Beyond the limits that have been imposed on us and take back our lives. Hanging off the edge of that cliff, chocking, I had to make a choice to hang there and give up the rest of who I was, or cut myself free and hit rock bottom, and I chose to hit the bottom.

The Affair

I crashed alone and was torn up, with skinned knees and a broken heart. A failure in my mind, a failure to my husband, a failure to my girls, and surely a failure to my creator.

It was at this moment that I gave myself permission to have an emotional affair. A long-distance romance with my best friend from youth. It was a bad decision, but finding out who you are doesn't come without pitfalls and mistakes. A beautiful October day, right before my 30th birthday, Dick broke it off with me for a real girl. Another crash landing into those rocks below. I had to find a way to love me without the strings and expectations of everyone else. It was a walk through dark woods with no path, just stumbling along the way and hoping that I would come across something familiar.

The Big Decision

I woke up in December the final year and decided I was finished. I didn't want to live in fear anymore. Fear that he might murder us in our sleep, fear of him hurting the girls. No more playing house, and no more faking it for the girls. I got an apartment and a bank account and came back with my decision already done. I would not be manipulated or talked out of taking back my life and the life of my daughters. I stood firm and just said it, out loud. "I got an apartment. We are moving out. December 30th will be our last night here." He was visibly shaken, and I know that in his mind he had no idea I could ever be strong enough to leave. "You are teaching the girls how to quit. Do you want them to think it is okay to leave your commitment just because you aren't happy?"

I laughed out loud. "I am teaching them that this isn't what a loving marriage looks like. I don't want them to grow up and think this is okay."

For me, the steps needed to leave were simple and fell into place faster and easier than anything that had ever happened in my life. Our apartment took my bad credit and deposit and gave me keys the same day I filled out the application. I had money to stay home for three months while I figured out how I was going to support my new smaller family. I had no job, no education and only so much savings to get us through, so each step of observing things falling into place made me stronger. They marked space in my life where I felt like I did the right thing by hitting the bottom instead of hanging on. Sometimes hitting rock bottom is the best place to build from.

The Right Step

The biggest sign, that I received confirming that I made the right decision is, the girls didn't care. They weren't upset at all, and they were actually excited. That pushed me on and drove me to take this second chance to become the me I truly was. To build a strong and stable life for them that was full of respect and hard work. Looking back, that can only be a true miracle that they made the path so easy. I had heard horror stories of kids clinging to the dad, sobbing, and questioning why. None of that happened to me.

I am not saying that it was smooth sailing after this. Separation and then divorce was hard. I made so many mistakes the first year we were on our own. I was still searching for who I was. I was disowned by most of my family, my husband tried to tell everyone that I was a cheater and a liar, that I kept his girls from him, even though none of those things were true. It hurts to have everyone look at you as the liar and the cheater. We can't be defined by those decisions, we have to see ourselves as God created us and gain strength from the knowing, that if we let him, he will guide our steps.

Self-Care

Several bad men decisions later, I decided I needed to work on me. I couldn't fill the void of my previous failed marriage through someone else. I needed to center my heart on God and what was important to him and focus on my daughters.

I learned that first year that I like John Mayer and I LOVE the Dave Matthews Band. I am not a fan of metal music, and I love art and poetry. I was a gamer and an artist. I learned that to truly be loved by someone else, I needed to love me for me. Learn who I was created to be and then love that person. That was the biggest challenge I had to get over. I learned that I had strong leadership skills in me, and that with or without a man I can provide for my kids and demonstrate true leadership.

When I had given up on the prospect of ever being a wife again, and no longer wanted to indulge in the responsibility of being in a relationship—I stumbled upon Joseph. My upgrade husband, when I had first met him months before that, he was this nerdy, twitchy guy working with me at Starbucks. He was living with his parents and working toward his Software engineering degree, the most unqualified man ever for someone to want to date or marry. He was the perfect friend though!

A New Relationship

We would hang out at my house after the kids went to bed, and watch cartoons and just be. It was the weirdest thing because I felt totally at ease with him. Sitting on my sofa in my tiny apartment, he used what had to be the best pick up line, EVER. "Friends totally snuggle." Laughing I said, "I totally didn't know that! Are you telling me we can sit here commitment free and snuggle and I don't owe you anything? Done!"

We became better friends and the occasional texts turned into daily texts, and then daily visits. His toothbrush, clothes, and other items slowly migrated to my apartment. But he still wasn't "living" there. Eight months into our relationship one night, Joseph and I stayed up way too late. We didn't want to end our evening. We had clearly become attached. We watched comedy videos until midnight. He had school and I had to be up at 3 a.m. for work the next day but admitting bedtime meant he had to go home and neither of us wanted that. He looked at me, illuminated by my computer monitor and said, "I don't want to go." My reply, "Then don't." He stayed, another piece of the puzzle of trusting each other slowly with more and more of our hearts and our commitment. He never left after that. More stuff made its way to what became our apartment, and at the end of that first year, we were looking forward to more.

One day after an afternoon lunch, as he was headed out to class he turned to me and said, "I can see myself spending the rest of my life with you. But I don't know about marriage." I never thought about marrying Joseph, because I knew it wasn't something he ever wanted to do. Despite my younger girl dream to be a wife, I knew in his mind it wasn't a possibility. I knew that I loved him and the love and grace he showed me was real. For me, it didn't matter. As time kept going we had many late night talks. One included Joseph asking me what I wanted to do. What was my big dream? At that moment, I wanted to teach photography, as a professor at a university. There was a pause as if he was considering what to say next.

"Professor Tompkins. I like that." He said. "Wait, say that again?" My shock was thankfully covered by the evening darkness. This man who had just a few months ago said he didn't know about this marriage thing just replaced my last name with his!

The next months proved his devotion and commitment.

His parents weren't too keen on me in the beginning but he didn't care. Honestly, I didn't exactly look like the prized catch for their son. Divorced single mom of three doesn't scream ideal. But he was all in for me and the girls. And I was determined to prove I was the best catch any man could get lucky enough to have. *I finally believed in myself.*

One thing I have learned is that sometimes you do have to prove yourself. If you believe in yourself when the opportunity presents itself, you'll take the leap and show what you are made of, that you believe you are worth it, and you finally are. I have proved myself worthy of Joseph. And I truly believe he is my gift. If God gave me nothing else in this life, just to be his wife and watch my girls grow would be enough for me.

When you face divorce and the consequences that follow, it isn't easy. Some people will judge you, you may find yourself without the friends and family you thought would stand by you. The one thing that got me through each step forward, and each step back was that God had a plan for my life. If I closed my eyes, and let him lead me, the path would be carved out for me. I just had to let him lead the way. Sure, you will trip and fall. But he will help you stand up again, dust off your clothes, bandage those knees and keep going.

My journey has taken me through so many different directions. From growing up in poverty to being a well-off wife, to being a divorced single mom, I wouldn't change a thing. Each moment helped mold me into the woman that I am today and I am grateful for the adversity because it brought me here, to share with you the hope that divorce doesn't mean your life is over. It means you have a chance at a new beginning.

Tiarra's Transformation

Tiarra Tompkins is Vice President of OnFire books and

Managing Director for The Conversation Event. She has been coaching authors, speakers, and world changers on creating their legacy for over a decade. She is married to her amazing upgrade husband, Joseph and has three beautiful daughters, Faith, Aimee, and Sarah. Tiarra is aware that everyday real conversations and words change not only the lives of her family but everyone they touch. Through her work at *OnFire Books* and *The Conversation Event,* Tiarra helps connect world changers and thought leaders, side by side with Tammy Kling to build companies that use words and real conversations to change lives for 1000 generations.

Reflection

By now you should be seeing a common thread, all authors took inventory of their inner self and steps to transform and blossom. In Tiarra's case, she came to the place of awareness that she needed to first love herself before she could love anyone else. Due to her toxic marriage, her self-confidence crumbled and that's what happens with any kind of abuse, it's like slowly chipping away at an ice sculpture, each shaving removed slowly widdles away our inner beauty leaving us with a low self-esteem and fear. Until Tiarra clearly identified that she jumped from one relationship to another trying to fill her inner void, she couldn't find love and peace inside herself. Bravo to Tiarra for recognizing this and making a shift, there are people in their 70s that I met that still struggle with this.

Tiarra through her healing had a better mindset; that whatever we put our minds to we can achieve and when the right person shows up in life to be your partner, the relationship will flow with ease.

Chapter 7

RISING UP

Bad things do happen; how I respond to them defines my character and the quality of my life. I can choose to sit in perpetual sadness, immobilized by the gravity of my loss, or I can choose to rise from the pain and treasure the most precious gift I have—life itself.

—Walter Anderson

When life sideswipes us depression and despair often takes hold and it can be crippling. It feels like everything is spiraling out of control and our environment is filled with chaos leaving us dazed, confused, and hopeless. When moments like this hit, we have a choice to feed into the destruction or press in, take charge, and control of our mindset and heal. After all, if thoughts can create miracles than just imagine how positive ones can transform a painful divorce.

Take a moment, step back, and realize that these life-changing moments are not what is happening to you rather what is happening for you. This is life's wake up call, to teach you something about yourself, that you are amazing, an opportunity to set a new course if you let it, a fulfilling life, and one far beyond what you ever dreamed of.

So when tough times hit it's important to focus your attention inwards when you feel stuck; close your eyes, silence your mind, and ask your innate wisdom in a deep state of contemplation, "what positive emotion do I need right now?" Then, "what step do I need to take to gently move forward in the right direction?" This will prevent you from taking on too much and becoming overwhelmed which will lower your self-esteem even further. It's important to enter a space of non-judgment, one that doesn't point the blame at others or your circumstance. It takes practice and the more you practice, the more things flow and you suddenly become unstuck, shifting from un-fulfillment and pain to a position of self-empowerment and joy. Move forward slowly, have the courage and be willing to step outside of the boundaries that are locking you in and leaving you unfulfilled. Your inner chemistry will shift from pity and anger to gratitude, compassion, and forgiveness.

This is your chance to turn your obstacle into an opportunity, to shift from a place of feeling depressed and challenged to transforming into a radiant soul that inspires others. Causing you to open up to your full potential, an opportunity to find out who you really are.

From Pain to Purpose

The Shattered Marriage Dream

As a little girl, I dreamt of my fairytale wedding, the princess dress, the horse and carriage, I was always excited about getting married, having kids and living happily ever after. I just had to plug in the Prince. I actually started my wedding scrapbook in high school; dresses, flowers, and locations. Talk about terrifying a boyfriend quick if they found that!

At 28 years old, I entered marriage excited, in love and in awe of what life had ahead for us. I just knew it would be fabulous, and forever. After all, he had rescued me from a verbally abusive ex-boyfriend and stalker so it seemed, my Prince had arrived. Jon was a bright energy with an even brighter smile. He was tall, dark and handsome, along with athletic, funny and laid back. We laughed a lot and played a lot as we were both college volleyball players. We were the couple to beat on the courts! Life was easy in those early days. But 28-year-old me, didn't recognize this "Knight in Shining Armor Syndrome," I'd placed him on a pedestal he was bound to fall from all too soon.

Jon entered my life at this pivotal time when I was in need of a shift. But I needed to find that shift from within and not externally. I poured my energy into helping him find direction and goals for his career. I saw such great "potential" for him. If he "could just" and "would just" tweak a few things; be more motivated, be more responsible, be MORE...you get it! If the now 50-year-old self would have been talking to 28-year-old me, she would have said, "He's not your semester project, he will be your husband for the next two-thirds of your life, maybe 60+ years. He will be the father of your children. You're in love with his potential, not with who he truly IS!"

Who knew that 50-year-old me was wiser than this girl?

But I don't think that girl would have listened anyhow. That girl believed that with enough love, anything is "fixable." So when the dream of "my forever marriage" came crashing down around me, divorce becoming a reality, it shook the foundation of my beliefs. "Marriage was supposed to be forever. Love conquers all. After all, I'd given and made endless sacrifices, how could he not love me or our son enough to be the man and father he needs to be to save our marriage?" I took the weight of his decisions, his shortcomings and his neglect upon myself and personalized it. My trust was conditional upon his behavior and our changing environment.

Every marriage goes through turbulent times, it is how we deal with these times together that determine whether we arrive safely at our destination or we make a crash landing needing the black box to help understand where our navigation tools failed us. Our marriage may have endured a few extra storms that were out of the norm but our navigational tools and communication skills being so different is what caused our ultimate crash.

Soon into our marriage, Jon got very ill and was unable to work for over a year. My parents and I were his sole caregiver's, which he seemed to be bitter about instead of grateful for the care and love he received. His personality was shifting quickly as depression crept in. Our marriage suffered financially following years of spotty jobs and unemployment. I'd attempt to "fix" things by financing his schooling, his startup ideas and a new business. I tried to help motivate and inspire him to tap into his best self. I even went to a married couples retreat (alone), to help heal our marriage. That was interesting! But I couldn't row this boat with one paddle. It was not within my abilities to fix him, he had to want to fix things, it was his job to make that shift from within, just as it was my job to stop being an enabler. My external influence was only making him dig his heels in deeper.

We had been married for five years when I finally decided to jump on the dream of having a child. I was waiting for our financial situation to improve his employment before having a baby. I'd hoped being a father would spark motivation. They say there is no perfect time to plan for a child and at 34 my biological clock was ticking loudly. Especially if we were going to have multiple kids like our "original plan" had been.

At 35, Gabriel blessed our lives. I gave birth to our beautiful blonde-haired, blue-eyed baby boy. I was looking so forward to having time off with my child as I had been working two jobs and Jon was finally in a good position. Three days after our son was born, Jon lost another job! I was just crushed! Not only did I have a big recovery ahead from the C-section and infection, but my time home with Gabriel would be cut short. I had to return to work sooner than expected because our expenses were greater, as were our responsibilities.

Jon became the at home dad for the next several months while I quickly returned to work. I had recently been promoted to a Regional Manager in Pharmaceuticals and my career was on a fast track. My promotions and accolades were causing more descent at home as the verbal abuse and emotional neglect grew.

They say when tragedy hits it happens in three's. More turbulence hit our family with sudden and emergent health crisis for both Gabriel and my mom. Gabriel had a spontaneous cerebral bleed at three months old. From three months to two years, we had to do everything possible to make sure he wouldn't cry, concerned that any cranial pressure could trigger additional cerebral bleeds. At two years old, he was finally considered stable. At the same time, my mom was diagnosed with stage 3 melanoma, then a year later diagnosed with breast cancer. We were at a low point when the final blow came and we lost our home!

Jon, Gabriel and I had all been experiencing significant health challenges. I was concerned it was something in our home. The tests confirmed our house was invaded with black toxic mold. For our own safety, we packed only a few belongings and moved out overnight. Leaving many things behind because of contamination.

Turbulent times can do one of two things; it can bring you closer, by helping you evaluate what's important in life. Or it can divide because you don't communicate through the crisis. Our continued turbulence was heading us skidding off the runway quickly. Our polar opposite responses to stress were a continued division.

For two years, I would wake up every night in the wee hours

of the morning and evaluate if I should stay in my marriage or end it. Fears, lies and external noise conflicted my thoughts and interfered with the decision to stay or go...

"Life will never be the same."

"You made a commitment."

"Your child will be damaged forever."

"You can't make this work!"

The crazy me was evaluating; either I stay and we have another child or I get a divorce. Talk about conflicting thoughts! We had gone to a handful of counselors and having another child was always at the forefront of conversation. I wanted another child but wouldn't move forward with pregnancy until he stepped up to his responsibilities as a father and a husband. I wanted to give my son the gift of a sibling. I grieved this loss. The fog of fear lifted and I had a revelation, it's not about MY happiness, it is about the foundation of what I'm teaching my son of what love and marriage look like. I'm not showing my son what a marriage with teamwork, respect, compassion, honor, integrity, and love are about. By staying it would be a disservice to what he deserved to see, to know, to experience and to live. The pain and loneliness of staying exceeded the fear of the unknown. With grace, dignity, and respect, for myself and for one another, it was time to learn how to be unhitched.

We made an agreement when we took our marital vows; to be our best selves, to look after the well-being of one another and our unborn children. When I finally realized that staying in this marriage was not fair to my son, I was not my best self and we were not our best together, the time had come. I no longer had the respect or desire to continue to fight for a marriage that was so empty and lonely.

I entered marriage with the vision that we would live happily ever after. This was no longer our truth. My heart was crushed to see our home divided. I grieved deeply for my son. I grieved for the children I yearned to have. And I grieved for the end of a fairy tale that never was.

Letting Go of the Marriage

Nine days after he moved out, I filed for divorce, it happened to also be Valentines Day. Poignant but not purposeful! We decided any differences we had we would settle based on what was best for our son, not our own needs. We remained amicable, respectful, and supportive, and still are to this day.

I told Jon that he had six months to get it together until our divorce was final. If some changes were made and I saw a commitment to our marriage, I would reconsider. Needless to say, our divorce was final six months later. Reality hit him when he saw my new boyfriend, leaving my house and passing him in his bright yellow Porsche. Jon pulled up to my house desperate, as though he didn't know what had taken place the last several years of our marriage. His tears flowed, the regrets followed, the promises to be a different man were made, but it was all too late. The damage was done. It was time to move on and to forgive.

Self-Discovery

After my divorce, I was walking down a new path of discovery, being a single mom and sole provider with a flourishing career. I was the only divorced parent of my son's friends, his soccer team and his classmates; I lived in "Married Ville." Life was exciting yet painful finding our new normal of singlehood. All of my local friends were married, having couples dinners and couples outings, etc. It was evident that I was in need of expanding my circle of single sisters. It was then that I accepted a transfer to another city, we were going to have a fresh start. Life was evolving quickly as I was navigating this new path of change. Our life and home had become so peaceful and drama free. We had our routine and it was all pieced together so perfectly. We were headed on an open sea of endless opportunities that lie ahead for my son and I. However, that was not the plan life had for us. Suddenly, those tranquil blue seas were hit by a tsunami with no warning. Within seconds, every dream in our vision was wiped out and annihilated with the devastating words, "You have metastatic liver cancer."

The Crushing Diagnosis

"This can't be!" I cried out. I have a four-year-old little boy, I'm a single mom and my baby needs me", as though I'm pleading for my life. My world completely stopped! Time froze. Every "What If", you could think of was coming at me as though I was trapped inside a hornet's nest swatting away these words while being attacked and stung from every direction!

Gabriel and I went from a tranquil sea of possibilities to being dropped into battle with no way out. This is a war that we had no idea how to fight, our only weapons are faith and hope. My biggest fear wasn't dying, it was leaving behind my little angel Gabriel, an innocent four-year-old little boy that needed his mommy to teach him, to guide him, to love him, and to LIVE!

The doctor told me my chances of survival were minuscule, with six to twelve months left to live. Searching for second opinions, another doctor told me it was time I get my affairs in order. I vowed to do anything I could to fight this cancer as my son needed his mommy. We had just started a new journey together and it was supposed to be full of light and love. He needed me here to teach him so many things that life had ahead of us.

The light that illuminated my path and gave me the strength and perseverance to fight with every breath I had, ended up being with me all along, my light was Gabriel and God. Through this cancer journey, I discovered so much about myself, about others, about love, and about loss. Cancer has a rippling effect as it touches not only the fighter but all of those within their circle, whether they like it or not.

There were many highs and many lows during this battle. Times filled with light and times of darkness, a darkness I never knew existed. Some of the darkest hours would visit me between 2:00 and 4:00 a.m. A deep loneliness would enter my heart, awake in my bed and alone with only my thoughts. Fighting cancer, facing death, feeling sick, all while hearing my sweet child breathing and dreaming across the bedroom that we shared. Nothing was as lonely as these hours praying that the Lord spares my life so I can raise my child and he doesn't have to suffer. Middle of the night, journal entries and writing letters to my son should I not live to see his many firsts; his first day of school, his first crush, endless firsts would be missed. It is real, it is raw, and it is painful!

When this kind of darkness creeps upon our hearts, we must remember that darkness is only the absence of light. If we seek the light, we will find it. In those hours, I knew the sun would rise soon and with every sunrise is the promise of a new day that is full of hope! It is within the darkest skies that the brightest of stars will shine. These stars were rays of love and hope. I found so much love and hope within my cancer journey because I looked for it. Cancer steals so much away from us but it also gave me gifts I'd never expected. There are conversations I was blessed to have that may not have ever taken place, because I was facing my death. You are truly living in the present because you're absorbing every sound, sight, and moment as though you are experiencing it for the very first time. Cancer allows you to recalibrate what is important in every aspect of your life.

I came to the realization that if I was to die, how I continued to live through this battle mattered, I didn't just want to survive, I wanted to thrive! I wanted to witness and be a part of the joy of my son's every breath, every giggle, every tear, and every tiny bug he stopped to observe in wonder. I wanted to live in the magic of life's every gift. Fighting cancer allows you to make that choice because you have a new awareness. Cancer may eventually take your physical body but it can only take your spirit if you allow it to. No matter what my outcome was to be, I wanted to embrace life's every gift and inspire others to do so as well.

The biggest message that I wanted to share was to live and breathe the gift of love and hope. It was a beacon of truth for me that love is why we are all here. To give and to receive love; in its many forms, in its many lessons, with its many gifts, and its many losses.

The plan to beat this cancer was backed by love and would be a long, uphill battle. When you are told you have only a few months to live, the last thing you want to do is be away from your child. But that was the sacrifice and gamble I had to make in order to find my best odds at survival and a treatment team that spoke the words of hope. I traveled for a year from California to Houston for what seemed like an endless array of treatments. Over the year, I endured; chemotherapy, surgical removal of 80% of my liver, gallbladder and lymph nodes, then a combination of radiation and chemotherapy.

A String of Miracles

Had it not been for the gift of love, I wouldn't have been able to travel to Houston in search of my miracle. I was surrounded by family, friends, co-workers, and strangers that came together as a community to help me with my child, costs of travel, my job, fundraisers, prayers and a healing vigil. Love and hope was the foundation of my fight. Love and hope are the foundation of my survivorship as I celebrate now over twelve years cancer free!!!

There are many things in life that will change you, but these three will change you forever: love, loss, and hope. Hope was my mantra for survivorship, for love, and for recovering from loss! I was still full of hope that "my forever" was out there and God's divine timing hadn't arranged this yet. But here's the conundrum; I don't do online dating, not interested in blind dates, I live in the country and when I am home, I enjoy being a mommy. I really only go out, when I travel for work or pleasure. So either I date an out of towner or I might be dating my local FedEx or UPS guy since that's whom I see. Since the divorce, I've had a few long relationships with quality men, who lived out of town. I enjoyed our time together but I knew they weren't mine forever.

One night, a very serendipitous encounter changed everything! Love walked through my door in a way that truly seemed to be a divine appointment. This chance meeting, created by the Universe, was a timely and intense connection. There were no accidents or happenstance in the way we met. If anything were off by a few seconds for the entire day or evening, our encounter would not have taken place. I felt his energy from across the room as his eyes were focused on me. He was a strong, handsome man with a regal presence and gentlemen's charm. Once that chance connection and conversation began, it didn't end. Our relationship began from that moment on and was a kinetic bond. Josh was a visionary and a creator all while being a humble and honorable ex-military man. We would spend hours in conversation, closing every restaurant we dined at fully engaged in dialogue, dreams, and discussion. Our chemistry both intellectually and physically was like nothing I'd experienced. I fully trusted him with my thoughts, my dreams, and my heart!

Fast forward I am now six years cancer free and believed God left me here for a reason that I had not yet tapped into. As the sole provider for my son, my stable career and good income were crucial to our well-being. But I kept hearing a voice telling me to move in faith and trust, to help children fighting cancer. Because of my relationship with Josh, I was inspired to actually follow this calling. With his encouragement, support and belief in me, I made the decision to start a nonprofit to help kids fighting cancer. We talked through the business and emotional aspects of it, night and day. I felt like it was a sign that God was telling me my day had come to leap off the corporate cliff! It was time to fly on the wings of hope! It's amazing what we can do when our passions meet a purpose greater than ourselves and are ignited by faith, trust, and hope. Because of that, I left a 14-year corporate career as a Regional Manager in Pharmaceuticals and founded the nonprofit, Along Comes Hope®.

The sacrifices I made were much bigger than I had originally realized. I left behind a very secure career, a comfortable lifestyle, and income. I gave back my company car, said goodbye to my benefits, my bonuses, and my paychecks. I ventured into a world of uncertainty with no paycheck, no benefits, no bonuses, and no company car.

My compensation package changed immensely; my

bonuses became miracles of a child being cured. My pay-checks became the deep gratitude parents would share at the difference Along Comes Hope® had made in giving their family hope and support.

My benefits became the smiles, hugs, and laughter I'd get to share with every brave child I encountered. My career went from receiving many tangible items of monetary value to ones that you cannot put a price tag on: Gifts of love, service, and hope!

Life really seemed to be piecing together so wonderfully. I had a career that allowed me to work with passion and purpose. My health was whole as I was considered cured. And I'd never loved a man as deeply as I loved Josh! For the first time ever, I felt like I could release the steering wheel and know he would take it over and keep me safe. He cared, he was there and I could count on him.

A Shift in Energy

Unfortunately, life doesn't always coast when it is set on cruise control. Suddenly, the energy with Josh began to shift, I could feel it from D.C to California. We had already faced a few painful breakups because of our long distance, but mainly because he wanted children and I didn't know about pregnancy due to my past cancer treatments. I was open to having kids by any means. But his sights were set on conceiving a child. The grief of wanting more children is surfacing again but now with a dynamic, I hadn't anticipated. I've always envisioned my life being surrounded by children and this contradiction was so painful.

Josh couldn't seem to stay away when we would break up. He would always find a way back into my life and I'd welcome him back with open arms and an open heart every time, believing he was back because *this time* he was ready for marriage. This became a long and painful cycle of highs and lows over four years.

Josh betrayed my trust beyond what I ever dreamed he was capable of doing. While seeing me, he simultaneously had another relationship with a married woman going for two years. In turn, she was cheating on her paraplegic husband that had recently suffered from an accident. She had left her husband and children for Josh. To top it off, when this was uncovered, they had just closed escrow on a new home they bought together and were now engaged. This was all taking place while he's making plans to go on vacation with me and continue our relationship.

I never believed he could be so deceptive and void of concern for others, let alone me. I always said, one thing he is not is a liar! My faith and confidence in my judgment of character were deeply shaken. I didn't understand how he could have no regard for my wellbeing. This was a pain I had never known. He tried to make amends, once I confronted him but his apologies fell upon deaf ears as he'd been caught. Instead of exposing him to his world and letting everyone know the truth, I remained quiet and disappeared from his life. Their relationship was built on lies and deceit and it is their karma to live with, not mine.

When betrayal like this happens, I think we often linger on searching for the "why" to help find closure. But often, those words never come and the "why" is left for us to release. We have to find our own way to move forward, heal the wounds and fill that darkness with light, which is where forgiveness lives.

When we love, there will always be a loss. Not because of failed love or intentional pain but because that is our contract when we entered this world. We are all a temporary presence in this world and the gift of our presence is determined by the risks we are willing to take. The gift of love can't be received to its fullest unless you are willing to give it to your fullest capability. We often walk this earth in such fear of ever being "hurt like that again" that we shield our hearts, which inevitably blocks us from fully receiving the endless gifts that love brings to our world. I can now say, I am thankful I was able to love him so deeply and I will love even more deeply again, when "my forever" arrives.

Gazing in the Mirror

Have you ever had a dialogue with yourself and it actually made sense? This conversation was not just with my reflection; it was with the girl in the reflection, who only yesterday, was 20 years old. That girl was filled with dreams, endless summers, and years of life ahead of her, it didn't seem like much of my life evolved the way I had meticulously planned. There are flashes of guilt and sorrow for precious years that seem lost due to unforeseen changes, decisions, and times of great loss whether that was of love, of health, of what was, what is or what was supposed to be. I was living in a past place of pain but I didn't recognize it until this gift of clarity surfaced.

I'm never one to be weepy about my birthday, as I was told I would not likely see the age of 39 due to a diagnosis of cancer, so every birthday is a gift to me. However, the morning my 50th birthday arrived, I started it off with that painful conversation in the mirror while getting ready to head to the gym. Hitting 50 seemed exciting as it was actually going to be a fresh start, especially because I was recovering from being bedridden for months due to an injury and surgery. I'd promised to make this an era of new beginnings. I didn't know just how "new" of a beginning it was going to be.

Mid-workout, a sudden flow of tears began streaming down my face. This emotion of desperation came over me, "I want more time!" I said aloud to myself. People must have thought I was working out really hard since I was driving myself to tears!

This feeling of desperation, of the desire to redo, to start anew, to do more, to be more, stole my breath away. It wasn't just the elliptical taking my breath away! It was overwhelming because I didn't realize that I had packed away these emotions, these thoughts and desires. I was hearing and feeling that metaphorical clock ticking loudly. The number of days I had remaining here on earth is limited. "I WANT MORE TIME!"

Now to top it off, I had also decided to work out to country music for the first time ever in my life. Why would I work out to country unless I wanted to cry?

For some reason, I was inspired on this particular day and I immediately knew why when a song came on that had a message, just for me....

Stop starin' at the rear view
You ain't checkin' your hair
That wheel has spun and them lights are out
There ain't nothin' for you back there....
"The day that you stop lookin' back
You're gonna find that the future
Sure beats the hell outta the past....

This was a double confirmation, a sign that God has a message I needed to hear. This message quickly turned into an epiphany, a new awareness, and a gift to me. I needed to shift this line of thinking to mirror determination, not desperation. "Rephrase your thinking and your words"...So I did!

I want my time here to be full of love and joy. I want to

make more of a difference and impact in the lives of my family, my friends, and the world. I will be more, do more, and help more. Stop looking in the past (in that rearview mirror) for the answers. I won't see the road ahead if I keep looking back.

This wasn't coming from thinking I wasn't "enough", it was coming from knowing I wasn't living to my full potential. It was coming from this new awareness! I was still carrying around old pain and outdated, heavy baggage. The kind of baggage that doesn't have rollers or a handle for ease of carrying, this stuff wasn't a carry-on. Oh no, this is the old antique kind that is big, bulky luggage, the kind that our grandparents carried. Beautifully crafted, smooth leather-bound cases, lined with soft silky material, and smelling of musky memories. The kind that today, you would store your actual treasures in. Yes, I was storing some of my past hurts and keeping them held in this sacred place. Stored away as treasures when in fact they were limitations and barriers to my goal of having my time here on earth be more, more full of love and joy.

This baggage had become a heavy burdensome weight that was limiting my best me. It was a place I knew well and it had a perceived sense of security. I already knew who, what, where, when, and how these hurts materialized but I didn't always understand the "WHY" they happened, and that was where the pain was keeping me stuck. This residual pain caused me to block new opportunities; new love, new dreams, and a new story. It was beyond time to honor and release the pain and the lessons they provided in order to be open to the gifts that lie ahead!

It was time to check these bags to a destination I would not be heading to. If only it were going to be that easy to blame someone else, go buy replacement items for the trip, get a refund and be done. Nope, it was time to begin unpacking this sacred suitcase of a painful past filled with memories of divorce, cancer, grief, and heartbreak. These old hurts carry a repetitive theme of love and loss, trust, and betrayal and the healing power of forgiveness.

It was going to be a process in unpacking this present day baggage, and like any unpacking, it required doing laundry; saying hello to those old familiar pains and honoring them individually in order to forgive and heal. I start reliving, recalling, and recognizing my role within each one of these journeys. Seeing myself as an active participant, not as a victim. I thought I had forgiven but the residue still resting on my heart told me that I had not completed this most important task and aspect of healing.

Going Deep Within

The first item I needed to unpack was ten years of marriage. It was resting atop of everything in this suitcase. Like I'd packed away a dripping wet shirt, the moisture, and smell permeated the bag. As I unpacked the musty old pains of a marriage filled with broken promises and neglect, I found forgiveness in his humanness and flaws. I no longer personalized them being actions he took against me. It was his stuff and I played the enabler. I'm grateful for the gift of our child, which is the greatest gift of all. I learned and grew from our experiences. I always want the best for my son's father. Healing exists because of forgiveness. I am healed. I release you and I forgive you!

What I didn't see was that I had also become emotionally unavailable. I was subconsciously selecting partners that matched the energy I was giving out. My role in this never occurred to me. Once I separated from my husband, I was excited to be remarried again to experience a true partnership.

Why would I have become emotionally unavailable? I likely believed that if I didn't let anyone get that close, I couldn't be emotionally abandoned again. That was naïve!

There was not a crevice within this luggage that wasn't being flooded with light by this newfound truth and awareness. What shined so brightly was that my heart was still the biggest wound, the biggest wall, and the biggest warrior within this well-kept keepsake.

From the time I can remember, I've placed my trust and my heart in the hands of others. Needless to say, I was let down time and again. From broken promises to betrayal and abandonment, they are awakenings that people aren't perfect even if you have placed them unfairly on a pedestal of infallibility. The pressure and this level of expectation are too great for anyone to achieve success. It is a recipe for failure, for both of you. They will disappoint you, even unintentionally, as we are all human. We all make mistakes and we hopefully learn and grow from them. I just happened to personalize their mistakes, failures, and their humanness in their fall from grace. The mirror image of trust is forgiveness. I had yet to truly forgive and my trust remained conditional.

So it became clear that the next item to unpack, release and honor in my emotional luggage is one that has permeated not just the items in this suitcase but even those that have tried to help carry my bags for me. It is the lingering scent of grief and heartbreak. A scar that remains sensitive to the touch. The enlightenment and gift came in uncovering the WHY that Josh came into my life. His purpose wasn't to be "my forever." He helped me discover the bravery and confidence within to be of service to children fighting cancer. The love, honor, and respect we shared helped me make that leap of faith to start my nonprofit serving children in a cancer crisis. Now, children surround my life; and I am grateful and I honor his role in my journey. I am healed. I release you and I forgive you!

The final item to unpack and release in my old emotional baggage is resting just below that wet shirt of divorce. It is the looming smell and weight of a terminal cancer diagnosis, stained with loss and betrayal. Loss of love from those who are fearful of getting too close, because they could lose me to cancer and betrayal of those that disappeared when I needed them during my fight to survive. I know without facing such a fierce and life-altering battle that I would not be leading a life of service and leadership as I am today. I am a voice and advocate for many in need. I know my battle caused many to face their own mortality and that was a scary place they couldn't go to. I know some were not ready to be there for me in the way I needed them to be but that doesn't mean they don't love me. I am healed. I release them and I forgive them!

A New Attitude

The gift on this day wasn't just my 50th birthday; I was blessed with an awakening! Today was the day I was going to make peace with time! The best time of our lives is in the now, even if it is a time of pain. Right now is all we are guaranteed. Receiving a terminal diagnosis, I know better than to live any days of my life in regret or the perception that I have "wasted days." I know how precious time is, I had made it out of the rubble alive and I was no longer going to allow the debris of my past to cloud my vision and my heart.

Whether it is divorce, cancer, grief, or heartbreak, every one of us will experience loss in our lives. How we survive and thrive through the journey creates growth and your true win. May we all rise from the ashes of pain and celebrate our rebirth of the resilient and majestic, Phoenix. Fly high and live your forever today!

Words of Encouragement

Do not wrestle with time or your past. Make peace with time. The sooner you do, the more you will enjoy the gift of the present. Don't give energy to regret thinking any of your days were wasted. There were gifts within every one of those minutes, even if some were filled with pain, loss, or fear. The lessons learned in the darkness help you seek the cracks of light you're in search of. That is where the gifts, the joys, and the greater You emerges from the ashes.

Today Jenny Is Thriving

Jenny Mulks is a mom, cancer coach, speaker, international author, advocate, philanthropist, humanitarian, and a cancer thriver!

She is the Founder and CEO of Along Comes Hope®, a nonprofit organization helping families of children with cancer. Their mission is to provide support through financial assistance with travel for treatment, creative emotional support programs and advocacy to promote policy changes, awareness, and education.

Jenny has been mentoring cancer patients and caregivers since 2007, after she faced a rare and aggressive cancer, giving her only six to twelve months left to live. She has been thriving against many odds and is cancer free, for nearly twelve years now.

Leaving a successful, 14 year career, in the corporate pharmaceutical world to start a nonprofit serving children with cancer, she teaches others how to work through a cancer journey to a "Can-Serve" journey, by being in service of others and sharing the gift of hope.

As a Cancer Coach at "We Can-Serve Together: Thriving Through Cancer." Jenny's online courses provide guidance to cancer patients and caregivers serving as a liaison between the practitioners and patients to help them thrive during their cancer journey and align their mind and soul with their body.

Reflection

Wow, Jenny is truly a warrior she could have been crippled from the cancer diagnosis but instead, her mind and love for her son overruled and she survived. She truly is an inspiration to us all.

There are two key points that Jenny touched upon in her story, the first was searching for a man who later did not meet her expectations and as a result, she clearly defined that the search for love all along should have been within. We are programmed as a child to go out and seek what we want in life and that means trying to find our bliss in others. We are conditioned by our past and we seek to fulfill our expectations which are our way of seeking safety and comfort to accommodate the self-image we hold within and many times these expectations set us up for disappointment, the very thing we want to avoid is what we subconsciously invite into our lives. Once we remove the filters of perception which is what Jenny did in the end, it's then that we can see what is really happening. It took a lot of courage for her to go deep and self-analyze, embracing her irritations, she learned from the experiences and changed herself realizing that her journey was about her more so than others.

The second key point is infidelity, there are many of us that have experienced this in our past relationships and I am one of them. So, I am here to release you from the choice of your ex, as it's their karma to experience and deal with not yours and to explain why people cheat.

A sexual urge is one of the most compelling forces in existence. With infidelity, the sexual urge becomes so powerful that their attention is captivated by the energy causing sensual indulgence and ego gratification. When this urge is excessively used without real love, it progressively burns itself out, the search for pleasure through sex becomes an addiction to that person and progressively it disconnects them from the source of love within. When you become attached to someone through sex you not only become dependent on the other to love you but you progressively become incapable of loving yourself. When you lose your life force in a failed relationship and failed expectations, it turns into broken hearts and broken marriages.

*This is why often sex acts like a drug and
therefore it becomes as addictive as drugs.*

As a result, when you seek love from another person or the external world of objects and life situations, you are using your ego mind that is using your life energy that builds the love and harmony in your body and uses it to abuse your body.

*When you expect love from another person you automatically
disconnect from the true source of love within.*

Pure love is the permanent state of reconnecting with the subconscious spirit that restores the unity of love.

*The more you seek love from the external world and other
people, the more you separate from the outer and inner world
and suffer from loneliness and unhappiness that follows it.*
—Shri Amritji

Chapter 8

THE PERFECT LOVE STORY

Because I always have a choice, I choose love.

—Deepak Chopra

The secret to true unconditional love is shedding the mask of who we think we really are for this is not our true self. True love can't be achieved by holding on to expectations or silent reactions conditioned by our past that keep re-occurring in our present. So ask yourself, the memories and beliefs that exist in your mind, what validation do you give them?

It's time for a mind shift of focusing on being, accepting everything good or bad just as it is. When we remove the filter of our perception, we can see clearly what really is happening. This requires stillness, a moment of silence to hear what is taking place, what our thoughts are truly saying, a moment of shutting down from all external things and focusing on self with love and lack of judgment.

Reflecting on how unwanted things that have turned up in our lives, the very things we were trying to prevent are the things that have happened. The reality is that the more we control, the more fear of loss creeps in and the more fear creeps in the more of what we control moves from us and the farther and farther we move from our inner source.

The more conscious you become, the less of a cycle you experience and the further you move forward on your journey to awakening. You now make a conscious choice to grow and move forward with self-healing. You must not just embrace the irritation of what has happened but learn from the experience, this is what brings about change in self.

It all starts and ends with YOU!

When you feel unbounded and free that's when the healing begins, this is when you experience unconditional love. Everything we need to see is right in front of us. All we have to do is become involved in a close relationship with self and all will be revealed. When we do this there is more freedom of choice, creativity, loving, kindness, compassion, peace, and joy, we are becoming connected with self and all that exists.

Surrendering to Control

Divorce seems like such a decisive word. The dictionary defines it as a "legal dissolution of a marriage." It's meant to be a nail in the coffin for the couple and it seems so final, doesn't it? I've gone through two of them and let me state unequivocally they can be as different as night and day. And the recovering bounce back can be just as diverse. Most of your new world revolves around how the two of you respect each other after the fact. Let me explain.

My first divorce is what you typically hear about. A hot and loving beginning, struggles, kids, frustration, less sex, not always in that order, but most of the boxes get checked and then boom… You look at her and realize, there's no love anymore; in fact, there is hate and anger and more. Results? Bring in the lawyers and mitigate the damage. This is a painful and destructive process that thousands of couples experience every year. The road to recovery or thriving again can be more or less depending on how fast you fall in love or finding some kind of substitute for what you thought you were supposed to get in holy matrimony. But when you're under 40, there are many trophy women out there, so you try to get back in the saddle and give it another go.

After my first marriage, I had resigned myself not to get married again. I mean, what was the point? The marriage had become a nasty word with a whole bunch of negative side-effects and I didn't want to be in that space ever again. I had children, I was doing very well financially, could be with several different women who were happy to spend my time and my money, so marriage just didn't seem to be in the cards. Plus, I was very happy being alone most of the time and had no reason to want "more", even though most of the women did. Bottom line without my ex-wife around, I was thriving, but to be honest, I was searching. After the end of my first marriage and a decade, a couple of so-so relationships and a hole in my soul, I knew there might be room.

Dating Excitement

By that time, I was living in Toronto and coaching a University Men's volleyball team. It was Christmas break and time to relax. Each year the team would alternate between California and Florida to spend the holidays in the heat. So there was a lot of beach volleyball, regular gym workouts, some informal games with US university teams, beach, beer, and babes. Just a great way to celebrate the birth of Christ. We were like a big family, playing and cooking, hanging out on the beach, watching a lot of sports and just being guys. Because they were all hunks and good athletes, everywhere we played attracted bikinis and other interested parties. And adding to the mix in our motel condos, there were two swimming teams from Ohio, a synchronized swim team from Michigan and one other women's soccer team from Pennsylvania with coaches and several adult male and female chaperones. So, there was always something cute and vivacious to look at.

The difficulty for me was that my boys were between 19 and 24, while their old coach was over 40. So as far as getting together with the opposite sex was concerned, I was ancient and one can only talk about their kind of activities for so long without wanting some adult conversations. And even though there were some female coaches from those other teams, nothing seemed that interesting. And that was ok. My boys tried their best to get me hooked up, but the reality was I wasn't even in the ballpark. So I was happy just to watch them have fun and joined in on the jock and girl talk. But here is where it got interesting. I'm a spiritual person and for a couple of days after Christmas, I started having this real strong urge that I was going to meet someone. Now I didn't know who, or what that someone was, whether it was a man or woman or anything else. I just know that I had this feeling inside that someone important was about to enter my life. No other details came with it.

As it turned out, the next day was New Year's Eve and so we were all going to a local club to party. Well that afternoon, the feeling got a whole lot more specific, to the point where I shared my thoughts with several of the team. I said. "I have this real strong feeling I am going to meet a very important woman tonight." They all supported me as we got ready to hit the floor for the dancing and drinking. I left with huge expectations and a kind of anxious giddiness that I hadn't felt in years. All night different guys would come up to me and point to a woman and ask. "Is that her?" or "What about her?" I was on the hunt and eager to fulfill this premonition, but each and every woman I saw or who saw me was met with "I don't think so." Time was moving along and by midnight and the countdown, some of the guys had hooked up, but for me, it was just another empty night with my drink. I toughed it out till about 1:30 a.m. Then decided to pack it in. All alone and disappointed, I walked home thinking that how could I be so wrong about this feeling I had for days leading up to tonight.

I went to bed and fell asleep dazed and confused by my disappointment. When I woke up, the mystery was a memory and I'd put last night out of my head, chalking it up to some kind of spiritual misdirection. Today was our last day and we were packing up to leave very early the next morning to drive up to New Jersey to train with Rutgers for five days before crossing over the border. The guys were all asleep, so I went for a walk along the ocean. I thought I might get some kind of closure about this mysterious woman that I never met. But as I dipped my toes into the shallow waves, I didn't get anything from beyond other than a bit of a headache from the alcohol and lack of deep sleep.

When I returned, a couple of guys had emerged from the bedroom and had turned on the TV. There were going to be Ballgames all day and there was still some beer to drink and cold pizza. God Bless the digestive system of young healthy males. Breakfast of champions, I guess. Anyway, it was closing in on 2 p.m. and we were going to cook up a big turkey for our last meal, so I grabbed a couple of the boys and headed over to the local Piggly-Wiggly for supplies.

Unexpected Timing
Once back, most were now up and watching football. I put

all the supplies into the fridge and noticed I'd forgotten to get more milk. As it turned out, we were right across from a 7–11, so I decided to go grab a couple of jugs. As I got the parking lot, a woman came out holding a tennis racquet and a bottle of water. Now I assumed that she was one of the chaperones from other teams that were in our building, so as we approached, I was thinking she was cute and why I hadn't seen her before. As we got closer to each other, something grabbed me and made me walk directly into her path. Usually, as two people approach, both move to the side so you can pass, but for whatever reason, I did not do this and neither did she. So, we stopped basically face to face.

Now I told you I was spiritual, but without even a thought this is what came out of my mouth. "Where have you been all this time?" The words kind of surprised me as they cleared my lips. She didn't flinch and our eyes locked. Her response in a foreign accent was. "Where have you been?" Well, there we were, less than a foot separating us, both asking the same question. I couldn't quite place the accent, so I blurted out. "What accent is that?"

She replied. "I am Slovak."

I was a little puzzled. "Czechoslovakia?"

"Yes."

"So what are you doing in Florida?"

She smiled. "I am here with my daughter on vacation. We have rented a beach house down the road."

Why aren't you in the south of France or the Algarve in Portugal?" I asked.

Because I live now in Canada."

"Canada?" I said with a huge surprise on my face. "Whereabouts?"

"Toronto."

"Whereabouts in Toronto?" I went on.

"Near High Park. She said. "Why?"

"I live in Toronto too. Used to live in High Park, but now live in Oakville."

We stared at each other for a few moments digesting the information until she broke the silence with.

"I'm Teresa."

I replied. "I'm Regg."

We shook hands.

"Nice to meet you." She dropped my hand and asked. "So what are you doing here?"

I told her about the volleyball team and our Xmas break tradition. She said her daughter was 16 and a volleyball player and that they were both fans of the game.

Well, I was smitten with this woman, fascinated by her aura, and wanted to engage further. So I suggested that she and her daughter join us for our turkey dinner. She giggled and asked if I could actually cook. To which I immediately replied, "of course. I am a great cook."

We spent a few more minutes chatting about whether that was a good idea or not, but at the end agreed she would ask her daughter to come over. She gave me her phone number and told me to call around 5 and she would let me know then. I gladly took it and watched her leave before going into the store to pick up the milk.

Back in my condo, I talked to one of my boys and told him I had just met a woman in the parking lot and had invited her and her daughter for dinner. He smiled and asked how old the daughter was and if she was cute. What else should I expect from a 20-year-old? Then he asked me if this was the woman I was supposed to meet last night. It hit me then and there that perhaps this could be the case. So the next few hours were spent thinking about her and making sure the place was in some kind of decent shape to bring two women into.

At the stroke of 5, I was on the phone. My thoughts had fluctuated between whether or not she and her daughter would actually come. She saved me the problem by stating that she would indeed be coming over around 7. As for her daughter, she was uncomfortable to be in a crowd of strange boys. I said I understood and that I was glad that she would get the experience of my masterpiece, i.e., the turkey dinner. She said she was looking forward to eating a "man cooked" meal. So the date was on. Yoohoo!!!

We laughed about the cooking thing then hung up. I immediately went into the kitchen and gave the place a serious look. It was a bit of a disaster being our last day. But she was coming and that's all that mattered. I was going to finally get some adult conversation with a pretty good looking woman that I was intrigued by. I set the table, gave the bird a final basting, and settled in to watch one of the games. I would carve the turkey around 6:30, mash the potatoes, and everyone would start digging in.

At five to seven, I looked around. She might be here any minute and the joint was not conducive to the right energy. There were about 10 of my guys, half-naked strewn around the place drinking beer, with plates of food and loud cheering or jeering about each play as the games continued. This was not the right place to bring a woman for a first encounter. I looked outside and saw a car coming into the driveway, pretty sure it was her. I climbed down the stairs to intercept. She looked amazing. She had white jeans and a very pretty blouse and her hair had been let down from the tennis ponytail she had before. I was like a teenager and met her with a big smile.

"I'm ready to test your turkey." She said.

"mmmm," I mumbled. "I'm not trying to hedge here, but there's nothing but a bunch of teenage testosterone watching football up there. I don't think it would be appropriate to drag you into that."

I could see her thinking about it. "No turkey? So what do you suggest?"

"Do you drink Southern Comfort or Coke?"

She nodded.

"Then why don't I grab that and a plate of the bird and we go down to the park, eat, and talk there."

"Sure." She said. "Why not?"

I ran in and grabbed what was left of the booze and a six pack of coke, jammed some dark meat, potatoes, stuffing, some cranberry, and a pickle on the plate, then returned to her car. We drove down to the park but it was getting dark and the path to the beach was in the shade. I offered up the food. She nibbled on a few things and told me it was tasty. That was good enough for me. I suggested we go to one of the hotels along the beach and talk there.

We ended up in two chaise lounges on the shore where we watched the moon come up and the tide come in while we both inhaled the salt air. We talked about each other's lives and where we'd been and what we'd done and how we both ended up in Toronto.

The hours passed like minutes, but the energy was undeniable. There was a strong connection. At midnight, I told her I needed to get some sleep as I would be driving one of the vans at our 5 a.m. departure. She drove me back. I looked at her one more time and then asked very politely if I could kiss her. She looked into my eyes and nodded. I leaned over and our lips met. Well, that kiss changed my life. It was like a kiss from a thousand years ago, perfect in every way. We kissed a couple more times. It got passionate and we ended up necking like teenagers for at least another twenty minutes. We exchanged numbers and addresses and committed to connecting back in TO.

The next day I was off to New Jersey. A couple of days went by and I called her. I would be back in a week, but she would be traveling in the US, so we postponed. Over the next month, one thing or another kept us apart and the visual memory was starting to fade. Then, as I was taking my team to a tournament out west, the flight got canceled because of weather. The team would overnight at some parents place and try to fly out the next day. I took a chance knowing she lived near the airport, so I called. She was happy to hear my voice and agreed to come to meet me for a drink. She told me she was driving a green Camaro. I gave her the departure door I'd be waiting by and we could reunite in about twenty minutes. Now Toronto in January is a lot different than Florida in December. The last time I was with her, we were both tanned and in summer clothing. Today's temperature was below zero. We kind of recognized each other but we were in heavy jackets, the tans were gone and because we hadn't taken any pictures, it was really weird. We were quite formal and decided to go for a drink at a hotel near the airport.

Now both of us were cautious because we weren't exactly sure how this was going to go. But after a drink and some okay conversation, I leaned over and said. "Why don't we kiss?" She leaned in. Boom! There is was again, that kiss from a thousand years ago

Wedding Bliss

From then on, the relationship flourished. Both of us had experienced terrible first marriages and had sworn off the other sex. But within six months and to the surprise of all of our kids and friends, we talked about getting married. Two months after that, we decided to go to the Grand Turk Island exactly one year from the day we met and get married under the blessing of the universe. No one was invited, not even our children

We spent two weeks in an oceanside villa that culminated in the most amazing ceremony you could imagine. The small staff created a floral altar for us while the local justice of the peace presided over the ceremony. We scripted our own vows that echoed our feelings. And as we placed the rings on our fingers, we spoke these words.

"With this ring. I give only to you. All of my heart, my soul and my life forever."

We consummated the event with a dinner at a very unique restaurant with two strangers that we'd recruited to be our witnesses. And so the most beautiful and pure marriage you could imagine took place on that day, on that island.

We were so in love that it made people nervous and uneasy. We kissed in public, held hands constantly, couldn't keep our hands off each other in public or private and even upset our kids about how mushy we were. We absolutely loved being together all of the time. I mean we lived together, worked together, traveled together, did everything together. In fact, if we were apart for more than an hour, we'd be on the phone talking like puppy love teenagers. It was fantastic. It got so bad that our kids, called us "one." In every possible way, we were joined at the hip, day in and day out. The passion was breath-taking too. For the first ten years of our marriage, we couldn't stop kissing, fondling, groping and making love to each other. It was addictive. The dopamine and oxytocin levels must have set some kind of record. If anyone else has had this kind of euphoria, then only those few will understand how absolutely fulfilling this kind of relationship can be and that you should do everything in your power to hold onto it.

Life's Turmoil

But then life kicked in and things began to change. About 14 years into the marriage, business pressures, family issues, personal compromises edged their way in and the whole endless love scenario began to show cracks. However, we were still hopelessly in love with each other, but the outside forces began to pull us to a place that if we were not careful, could pull us apart. We pushed on for another couple of years dealing with challenges, but through all of it, we still had our daily hand-holding walks, kisses, and affection. But you could feel the momentum shifting. Anger had reared its ugly head and there was frustration from the business along with stress as her company struggled to make ends meet. I quit my job for personal reasons and that only added to the pile. The pressure became immense. We were losing the fight, were very angry at each other to the point of separation.

One day after a significant argument, my wife decided to move out of our home and move in with a friend. We needed to cool off and get some perspective. She came by a few days later and told me she would be spending a girl's week up at a lake in Northern Ontario. I was hoping this time apart might give both of us some space to reflect. We also decided that we should separate until we could come to some kind of solution. Our marriage of late had been badly fractured due to both business and family issues. Both of these had caused a deep wedge between us and it became unbearable to the point of no return. All that love had somehow been taken away from us. Things got very cloudy.

We kissed non-affectionately and off she went.

The Accident

That day turned out to be a definitive moment in both of our lives. I didn't hear from her for over a week. Then I got a call from the girl that had taken her up to the cottage. My wife had been in a serious boating accident a week ago and they were afraid she might die. She had smashed her skull and fractured her arm in a speedboat accident. She had been in intensive care in a hospital, been unconscious at the time of the accident, but was now stable.

She told me that my wife had told them not to call as she didn't want me to see her in that state. There was still a lot of love between us, and I insisted to see her.

That meeting was the realization of how lives can change in a split second. You see my wife had been in charge of her company, over 300 employees. She made critical decisions ten times a day. But this massive concussion had reduced her to a completely different person. She now had post-concussion syndrome. Her head constantly buzzed or had rung. She had little energy. Her ability to think or make decisions was virtually gone as she struggled to remember or process information. In fact, the woman I had been in love with day in and day out in life and business for almost two decades was no longer there. She had become a shadow of herself in every way. Physically, you couldn't see much of a difference, but the woman that I married was totally gone. She needed personal care and constant medical assistance. After a couple of months living with her girlfriend, she moved into a separate apartment where she could have the medical protocols, peace, and comfort she needed. This was the reality of our future.

The Decision to Divorce

One day about a year after the accident, on one of our frequent walks she confronted me. "I am no good to you as a woman. I have no desires and cannot give you what you need. I want you to be happy so we should get divorced so that you can meet someone and have a relationship. We both cried and hugged, but decided it was the best thing to do. So we sold our house and wedding rings and filed the papers. I moved into a condo and tried to re-invent myself. She stayed in the apartment where her needs could be met.

Over the next five years, we stayed in close contact, trying to save some sort of what we once had, but the damage had been done. We were now living in different places and with different agendas. She was fighting for some kind of stability, some sort of normality. I was trying to redirect myself to creating income and survival in a world of business. We couldn't offer each other any real peace, but we could stay the best of friends and we were both determined to do so.

This tragic ending of a very beautiful marriage took a massive toll on both of us. After being "one" for so many years, living in a bubble and then experiencing the separation, then accident put both of us into a kind of coma as far as getting out there. We remained close but in separate worlds. To go from the euphoric love that we lived a day in and day out for 17 years, to this kind of numbness where both of us had died a bit was extremely difficult. We tried a few times to give each other up as the pain of not being together outweighed the pleasure of being apart.

The Update

It's been over ten years now and here's where we stand. My ex-wife has worked very hard to get her life back. Her head trauma and post-concussive syndrome are 90% gone. Although she has not been able to work, her life has become more enriched by spending quality time at the gym, with her friends, family, grandkids and traveling. She walks and works out regularly as exercise is fundamental to staying vital. She has also engaged in spirituality and it has given her strength and focus. Once she accepted that full-time work was out of the question, she changed her habits to things that she enjoyed and could do without the demands of business. She even started a small line of lingerie that several local high-end boutiques carry. So, despite our failure as a couple and in the face of a nearly fatal accident, she has learned how to thrive. She occasionally talks in front of other women who have been through tough times and always gives them an uplifting and inspiring talk on how to never give up and that no matter what life gives you, you must be thankful and happy because there are so many of us who have issues and problems beyond ours.

As for me? Well, I sunk myself into business after the divorce trying to regain some form of balance. Without my partner, things took a long time to round out. I got involved in several businesses, developed some patents and took them to market. The stress and frustrations of working with several investors nearly killed me. A year ago, I had by-pass surgery on the five arteries of my heart. The doctor told me, I was literally a ticking time bomb. Fortunately, I had no complications and the operation was really amazing. After the procedure, it took me about four months to start feeling like myself, but in those four months, I re-arranged my life. I dropped all companies, people and products that had previously given me stress. I only resigned myself to work with people I like and respect. I re-balanced my diet, exercise and lifestyle values, re-published my book on how the empowerment of women have created "female compliant" men. It's called *What's Happening To Us?* And it offers both men and women a beacon of hope for long-term love and acceptance.

So, the fact is that since the divorce, the spirit has been pulling and pushing on both of us. Through all the powerful forces we have been exposed to, a lot of them quite devastating, we have both come up for air and are living a happy and fulfilled life based on our individual love, care, and enjoyment. My ex-wife and I remain the very best of friends. We still go for walks hand in hand and we still know the universe has blessed us because we got to experience the kind of true love few do. We both understand that levels of love change as time marches on.

The difference is that we have entered into our later stages in life, intact and with the full support of each other in almost everything we do. If anyone can have this kind of relationship with another soul, then you must be one of the luckiest people on the planet, because that's exactly how we both feel about our thriving lives and the love we still share with each other. Although we've lost the passion that we shared through the early years, we've grown to love each other on the level of trust and care and that kind of later love may be more important as we age. The fact that we cannot live together or share life as we used to is not relevant. What is relevant is that our souls will always be there for each other. And both of us thrive on that.

I will leave you with three of my favorite sayings:

Disappointment in life is certain.
Suffering after the fact is optional.

Good Luck or Bad Luck is not a random thing.

You always get what you prepare for.

You are exactly where you should be in your life right now.
Embrace it

Today Regg is Thriving

Regg Miller was born in 1950, in Winnipeg, Manitoba, Canada. In his late teens, he moved east where he took a stab at modeling and commercial acting in Toronto, Montréal and Chicago, where he rose quickly to the top, ultimately becoming one of those familiar print and TV faces for over 20 years. In his forties, he went on to become a successful international marketing consultant in North America, South America, and Europe. Because of being married twice which both ended in divorce, he has faced all sides of relationships. Throughout the years, opportunities and experiences put him into contact with thousands of men and women who experienced the turmoil and sexual freedom of the 1960s, the rapid explosion of female rights and technology in the 1970s, and the frenetic hunt for material wealth in the 1980s. It is through these decades and people that he acquired his knowledge and current point of view on many subjects especially the confusion and harmony between men and women.

Reflection

Regg chose thoughts that were uplifting, he felt he was going to meet someone special and he was open to the possibilities, embracing the understanding that there is a component of time that didn't belong to him. He stayed in the vibrational feeling of meeting someone special and that's when his wife turned up. Despite external circumstances that transpired,

Regg learned along to way to forgive and not give in to anger, instead, he chose to love, he respects and cherishes the incredible miracle that his relationship with his ex-supplied and because of it even after divorce his relationship with his ex continues to flourish.

Chapter 9

MAKING THE SHIFT

Each day is a new opportunity yesterday is over and
done. Today is the first day of my future

—Louise Hay

There is one simple reason as to why so many breakups in relationships happen, lack of self-acceptance for whom we really are, the inability to love self from a heart position in most cases due to past experiences and lack of knowing how to process the information. We look externally for people to fill our voids and fulfill our dreams because we are not OK with ourselves so we search in the wrong places for the answers when in reality the answers are already within us. This leaves us angry, frustrated, confused, and eventually, a train wreck defeated from the beginning.

We get caught up with the story we play in our mind, and then when others don't behave the way we want them to we get disappointed and we harbor resentment because they haven't fulfilled the expectations we set in our mind. This is important to understand because it's easy to get caught up in lust or love. But until we understand this and embody it, loving ourselves with grace and accepting ourselves for who we are, we will keep repeating the same mistakes, experiencing the same self-destructive patterns.

Your whole life has been conditioned to find love from others and it's like you have been sold a false bill of goods. You have to break your conditioned thinking and it can't come from just telling your mind to think something different, you need an anchor to achieve it and that can only come from the continual search within.

True love is found within. When you accept self, all things change naturally. Once you do the work that is required to heal and become whole it's then that you realize that it was your ego mind that was deceiving you into thinking what you were looking for was out there and if you would have continued on that path you would have never found it

So, connect to the energy of the inner self not the outer of future happiness.

Unless you find love within you,
you will never find love outside of you.

A Fresh Start

The Year of Fear, Frustration, and Food Stamps

Meet me circa 2006. I was working as the Head of Make-up and a part-time beauty reporter for a CBS TV station, raising three children, married, overextended financially, and, like most women, feeling enormous pressure to have a perfect life! I wore the heavy mask of perfection and spent a good portion of my time worrying about what other people thought. Looking back, I think of myself as being a "poll-taker." I'd take a poll by asking everyone one else what they thought I should do before I could make a decision. Most of the time, it was my husband's decision that I relied on because I didn't trust myself to make the right choices.

I've always believed that opportunities present themselves right when we need them the most. My opportunity for growth came when I was invited to attend a workshop for women called "Expansions," conducted by a well-known Life Coach. I don't know what made me say yes to this event, as I was already managing a very full work and home schedule, but I remember feeling called to say yes and take this time for myself. I am so grateful I did because it was the first step in reclaiming what I had no idea I had lost.

The event was filled with one hundred women, including attorneys, executives, artists, and other professionals who wanted to improve their lives. We were asked to limit any distractions during our time together and be completely honest while doing this intensive work.

The first exercise we were given was to answer the question, "Who are you?"

"Well, that's easy," I thought. "I'm a make-up artist and beauty reporter, a wife and mom of three kids."

The Life Coach asked us to share our answers, and after hearing a few resume-type responses and seeing that we completely misunderstood the question, the coach prodded, "No, no, not your ROLES. Who ARE you?"

The room fell silent. We all seemed puzzled by this seemingly simple question. After seeing our confusion, she asked an even more audacious question, "What do you love to do?"

I had no idea. What do I love to do? Is she asking about my to-do list? At that moment, I suddenly realized my life was not about me at all, but about taking care of everyone else.

The coach continued, "What are your core values? What is your purpose? What are your dreams?" The first thing I thought was, "Is this woman on crack?" I have no freaking idea how to answer any of these questions!

The more questions she asked the clearer it became to me how little I knew about myself or what *I* wanted.

I started noticing that many women were brought to tears

by these questions. Some remained completely still, pen in hand with nothing to write. Feeling rattled and uncomfortable, my reaction was to run and hide in the bathroom.

Behind the comfort of a closed door, I took a long, hard look in the mirror and asked myself, "What in the hell happened to you?" I had no idea who I was anymore. I had completely lost myself in the roles I was playing and the mask I was wearing.

On the outside, my life appeared perfect: happy marriage, three healthy kids, a thriving career as a makeup artist, nice home, and a close network of friends. To anyone looking in, I looked like I had it all. On the inside, I was completely falling apart.

I was married to a man who I loved dearly but who had a major drinking problem. When he drank, he became verbally abusive. I kept thinking if I could just do more, he would stop drinking or if I could be more, he would love me. I had tried for years to make him happy, thinking I could *fix* him, but time and again, I failed. My marriage was crumbling and no matter how much I wanted to save it, I knew it was over. I also had three kids who were seriously over-scheduled because I had signed them up for multiple activities trying to maintain the image of the "perfect" mother who had the "perfect" kids. My husband and I were overextended financially with a lavishly decorated home to maintain the ever illusive "perfect" image of success.

During that workshop, I realized that nothing I had on the outside made up for what I was missing on the inside. If I wanted to be happy, I needed to tap into who I truly was, and I needed to be honest with myself. My marriage, my financial situation and what was truly going on in my life was not working for me. I made the choice that day to ditch the mask of perfection for an opportunity to discover who I was, and what my dreams and my values were so I had a real chance at happiness.

With any major life change, the first step is always the hardest. It was time to leave my unhappy and unhealthy marriage. Although after making the decision to leave my marriage, there was a slight sense of relief, this feeling soon evaporated and what followed was a tremendous amount of fear. I was terrified and trapped in fear on so many levels. Fear of letting go of the love I had and wishing it didn't have to end. Fear of not being able to take care of myself and my children financially. Fear of what others would think. Fear that all those awful things my husband said about me might be true. I knew, however, if I stayed, I would have to destroy pieces of myself that may never fuse together again, leaving me fragmented, torn apart and never knowing who *I* am.

Just when I thought I had everything under control, a situation arose that made me question my decision. Right after leaving my marriage, my boss called me into his office to tell me the station no longer had the budget for a full-time make-up artist. He told me, however, that he could offer me a job hosting their new morning talk show. At first, I was thrilled as this would give me the opportunity to be on camera, but I quickly learned that the salary was little more than an assistant manager on the night shift at an average fast food restaurant. While I was grateful to have this opportunity, I also knew that the small salary would make it impossible to provide for my kids. Having to support my family on my own now, I took this position despite the pay cut because the economy was taking a dive and this was not the time to go job hunting.

Every morning, I got up and painted on a perfect face and fake smile, and I wished the viewers a hearty, "Good Morning" before running back home to hide and cry under the covers. Remember the promise I made to ditch the mask of perfection? Well, here I was, all over again, creating the illusion of perfection, only this time, I wasn't fooling myself. As the divorce dragged on and my money dwindled, I soon realized, I was in deep shit!

I was scared, frustrated, and angry, and I felt like a failure for not being able to make my marriage work. I was anxious about letting my kids down and I worried about our future. There were even moments, although brief, that I thought it would have been *easier* or *better* if I had just stayed. I was, alone, with three kids to raise, with no energy, no hope and not nearly enough money to provide for my family. Too ashamed or proud to ask for help from family and friends, I had no other option but to apply for food stamps to put food on the table.

As I stood in line at the government office, my only wish was that no one would recognize me. Can you believe that was the only wish I could come up with at that time in my life? Even in that desperate moment, I worried about what other people might think if they saw me applying for food stamps!

Oddly, while in the government office, the celebrities I had worked with over the years came rushing to mind. Day after day, these gorgeous men and women would plop down in my makeup chair and point out everything that was *wrong* with their appearance and then ask me to cover it up. This request was usually followed by the problems they faced with people and situations in their lives. I couldn't see their flaws, and neither could anyone else for that matter. I only saw their beauty. In fact, the only person I didn't see the beauty in was myself. Why could I so easily see the beauty in other women, but couldn't see it when I looked at myself in the mirror? I tried so hard every day to create the image of perfection, but with every new effort, perfection only seemed to slip further away.

I didn't know who to turn to for help, and even if I did, the shame of my situation would keep me from reaching out and sharing how I felt. What I feared most was that someone would say to me what I had been saying to myself for years; I'm unlovable, I'm stupid for choosing the wrong man, I'm a failure, I'll never make it on my own. So, I did what most women do when in the throes of divorce. I suffered alone, in silence and I beat myself up over and over again. That mask of perfection was still running my life and keeping me from the greatest love I would ever know.

The Danger Zone of Emotional Bankruptcy

The first instinct after a divorce is to hide under the covers, eat buckets of ice cream, and cry, cry, cry. After the divorce, my self-esteem was shot. Like the rumblings of a blasted building, my identity was all but in pieces on the ground. Coincidently, one of my co-workers was going through a terrible divorce as well. We started spending time together talking about what we were going through and before we knew it, we were dating. For a brief time, I felt better. I felt beautiful and desirable again. However, deep down in my gut, I felt wrong about dating him for many reasons. For one, we worked together. Second, he was explosive with anger at times when he spoke about his ex-wife and when he talked to her on the phone. Third, he would tell me about how he chased her down in a car, ripped her to shreds verbally and more. I chalked all of his behavior up to heightened emotions due to their divorce. Red flags #1, #2, and #3.

Meanwhile, I was feeling very unsure about myself and this new role as a talk show host as I had no experience. It was not a good time to learn new skills on live TV in front of thousands of viewers every day. Over time, my co-worker/ new boyfriend helped me feel a little less insecure, yet in the process, he became more controlling in telling me what to do and how to do it. BIG red flag #4!

That's the problem with emotional bankruptcy. You do things, allow behaviors and ignore things you normally wouldn't. When you are hurt and feel down about yourself, the first person who comes along and tells you that you are beautiful and fabulous wins your heart. You begin to find a sense of worth you lost in yourself in someone else's eyes. But this reprieve is temporary and only brings to view all that you didn't want to see in the first place. Before you know it, you find yourself back in the same unhealthy and unfulfilling relationship cycle all over again. At least, that's how it happened for me.

Yes, there were red flags from the very beginning but the truth is I didn't want to see them. I didn't want to be alone… again. I was afraid that I wasn't capable of taking care of myself or my kids on my own. This is exactly why I married my co-worker and found myself in the very same type of marriage all over again…only much worse!

But this time, I was determined to do something different. I decided to seek counseling during my second marriage to help me figure out why I kept attracting the same type of man and the same type of relationship despite wanting something entirely different. This is when the real work began. It wasn't easy, it wasn't pretty, and it definitely wasn't fun, but it was exactly what I needed to begin the healing process.

Mirror, Mirror on the Wall

I had chosen two men who were very controlling and verbally abusive. I accepted their behavior, and quite frankly, overlooked it in the beginning. It took my second unhealthy marriage for me to see and understand that everything I experienced in the relationship had less to do with him and everything to do with me.

During one of my counseling sessions, the therapist asked me what qualities I wanted in a partner. What I wanted from someone else came easy and my desires flowed quickly from my heart. One thing was for sure; I was very clear about what I wanted in someone else.

After listing all of the qualities, such as unconditional love, trustworthiness, kindness, empathy, accepting me for who I am, the therapist asked, "Of all the qualities you've listed here, are you any of these qualities to yourself?"

Reviewing the list, one by one, I soon came to understand the real problem and it wasn't my husband—it was me! Not only did I not give to myself what I wanted from others, I would give everything to others to the point that I was totally depleted and pissed off, exhausted and in a crappy mood because I never took time to give to myself. I was looking for someone else and something else to fill the void only I could fill. What became painfully obvious was that my relationships, and in particular, my relationships with men, mirrored back to me what I felt and believed about myself. The only way I was going to have the relationship I wanted with someone else was by fixing the most important relationship I'd ever have—the relationship I have with myself.

Catching Myself in the Act

One day, holding so much pain inside and feeling like I might explode if I didn't release it, I sat in my car, turned on my phone camera and shared everything I was feeling in the raw.

No editing, no censoring, and no withholding.

I had been living with a very controlling man for years, When I was at my weakest, feeling anxious about an upcoming speaking engagement, worrying about my kids, fearing my father's imminent death from a battle with cancer, and utterly exhausted from trying to do it all, he would put me down, verbally rip me to shreds, and tell me I didn't have what it takes. The crazy thing was part of me thought I deserved this even though I knew his behavior was completely unacceptable. What made this so much more painful was I had written a book sharing the process I had learned and created to rebuild my life for women in this same situation! I was also teaching women how to love themselves, make themselves a priority in their lives, and build loving, healthy relationships; and women worldwide were completely transforming their lives through my book and coaching programs. Meanwhile, I couldn't believe how stupid I had been, to continually fall for this, and to tolerate this kind of behavior. How could I be doing the exact same things I teach women not to do? The simplest answer is that I just kept thinking he would change.

What came from that video was a mirror of everything I thought about myself - unworthy, unlovable, ugly, and stupid. I judged myself harshly, blamed myself for it all and instead of giving myself the support I sought from my husband, I beat myself up. I saw, for the first time, the deeply hidden beliefs I held about myself. That same day, I promised myself I'd dedicate my life to helping women redefine and rediscover themselves after a major loss. I knew the steps and what the process entailed and it was time for me to apply what I taught other women, after all, I needed to learn it the most. As the famous saying goes, what we teach is often what we most need to learn.

The Steps to Redefine and Rediscover Yourself

We all experience divorce in different ways, but there are significant similarities in what happens to us emotionally, mentally and spiritually. There is absolutely nothing to be ashamed of, and the feelings of failure, shame and loss are completely NORMAL. Major life changes, like divorce, offer us a tremendous opportunity to grow into a better, more complete version of ourselves if we are ready and willing to let go. Let go of the fears, let go of shame, let go of the limiting beliefs, let go of the desire to control others, and let go of the mask of perfection. Perfection is an unattainable illusion that holds you hostage. The harder you strive for perfection, the further away you'll get from the experiences, the relationships and the success you desire because you will be striving for something that does not exist, making your efforts fruitless and meaningless.

From my own experience and what I share with women as a Life Coach, we have two choices when we experience a major loss in our lives. We can look within, take inventory and ask what we need to change in how we think, believe, behave, and respond so we attract relationships, situations, and experiences we really want, or we can look outward, point fingers and waste a lot of time trying to please others and trying to control what we have no control over. The only person you ever have complete control over is you—your thoughts, your beliefs, your actions, and reactions. When you turn the mirror of experiences inward, you begin to feel the power you have over your life.

Honor the Process

When we decide to make a change in our lives, we tend to want immediate results. Making the decision to leave a marriage is no different. We've been feeling so bad for so long, we think that once we leave, we'll feel good again. The problem with this way of thinking, however, is that with any loss, a healing process ensures that it is neither instant nor linear. Just as there are stages of grief when you lose a loved one, so too are their stages of healing after a failed marriage. There will be times when you question everything from wondering if you made the right decision, how you'll get through the divorce if you are messing up your kids' lives, if it was all your fault, or if you are even worthy of a relationship at all. These questions are completely normal. You are moving from a place of certainty to a place of uncertainty, meaning you knew what to expect while married, but you don't know what to expect after divorce. I encourage you to give yourself time to heal through this process. Try not to judge, berate yourself, or numb yourself to your feelings. You'll know you're numbing yourself if you partake in numbing behaviors like drinking excessively or more than usual, smoking, or signing up for every dating site on the web. These are all forms of "not feeling" and in order to heal, you must feel. Also, don't let these feelings overtake you completely. Feelings, like everything else in life, change. Know that whatever you are feeling today may change tomorrow.

Say Hello to My New Best Friend

Remember that exercise my therapist asked me to do about listing the qualities I wanted in another? Now's the time for you to make your list and honestly ask if you give to yourself what you are looking to receive? Along with giving yourself time to heal, you need to love yourself through this process. You can practice this skill (and yes, self-love is a skill that requires practice) by doing mirror work, working with a counselor you trust, hiring a coach who understands what you are going through to support you, talking with a pastor or priest, or by maintaining a spiritual practice that includes journaling. Whatever way you choose to practice self-love, make sure you are consciously learning about you, your needs, and what changes you need to make in your thoughts, beliefs, and behaviors to heal and grow. How you traverse this path is not important; traveling the path is the key. This work is about forming a new relationship with the most important person in your life—YOU! Until you learn to love and accept yourself, you will continue to look outside for what can only be found within.

> *We are always doing the best we can*
> *with what we know now.*—Louise Hay

The first step to loving yourself is becoming aware of your thoughts and beliefs on a regular basis. We all have those things we say to ourselves that are less than kind, to say the least. We often offer kind words of encouragement and point out the strengths and beauty in others, but we rarely do this for ourselves. The truth is, we see the mirror of who we are when we see the good in others. Pay attention to what you say to yourself and what you say to others. Be sure to acknowledge that you did the best you could with what you knew at the time, just like everybody else.

When I was stuck in a cycle of shame and beating myself up, my life coach would say to me, "You're gonna pack that shit up in a box, carry it to the curb and let the garbage man take it away." Any time I got stuck in self-defeating doubts like, "what if I can't do this," "what if I never find love again," "what if no one ever loves me," or "what if I choose the wrong man again," I recalled what my life coach said and packed that shit up and took it to the curb. That's the power of awareness and having someone call you on your trash talk. And believe me, we all have shit that needs to be taken to the curb.

When you catch that little voice inside of you saying hurtful things, or telling you that you are not good enough, smart enough, pretty enough, etc., take note of those things you say to yourself. Ask yourself if this is how you really see yourself or are you repeating what you heard as a child or young adult? If you heard these things from someone, know that those words came from someone who didn't love themselves and really had nothing to do with you. If you find a negative thought or belief about yourself that you believe to be true, try to get to the root of that thought or belief. Perhaps there is something you need to forgive yourself for that you haven't been able to yet. Remember, perfection is an unattainable illusion. You are lovable just as you are.

Self-love takes practice. Just as you wouldn't expect a yoga body by doing one pose, one time, you can't expect to love yourself overnight, especially if you've had a pattern of self-loathing thoughts, beliefs, and behaviors. Love yourself through self-love. Give yourself what you would offer to a friend in the same situation. Treat yourself like your best friend and you will begin to attract people who treat you the way you wish to be treated because you will be showing them how to treat you by the way you treat yourself.

Every Big Change Starts with One Small Step

As a Life Coach, many women come to me with a host of changes they want to make. They want to feel better, look better, be more successful, find a partner who matches their expectation, find the perfect career, or radically change their looks. And they often want it all right now! Nothing will set you on a trail of failed changes quicker than trying to change EVERYTHING at once.

The first place to start is with loving yourself as you are right now. The next step is choosing one goal to work on at a time. Just one. As you make one small change, other small changes will begin to flow naturally. Whatever goal you set, whether it is regularly taking time for self-care, saving more money, or reinventing your wardrobe, focus on that one goal, create a plan to accomplish that goal and get support to help you stay accountable.

Trust Yourself

When I started taking tennis lessons years ago, the feedback I was given by my tennis coach was that I failed at following through. Every time I'd swing, I would simply stop mid-stroke. After telling me over and over again, "Follow through, Michelle," and seeing that I was not listening, he tried something different. He said, "Trust yourself" every time I went to swing. After a few times, something happened inside of me and I suddenly started following through on every swing. From that day forward, whenever I tried something new, I would say, "Trust yourself, Michelle," to remind me to follow through. When you trust yourself, you take action, and opportunities appear that support you in achieving your goals. When you trust yourself, fear loses its grip and a sense of confidence takes its place. Trust that whatever change you wish to make in your life, you have what it takes to see it through if you follow through. Trust forms when you follow through on promises you make to yourself. Trusting yourself means knowing you can count on yourself in all times and all situations.

Committing to one small goal, dedicating your energy and trusting yourself to follow through will reap rewards beyond anything you can imagine right now. And the coolest thing about this is as you strive for that one goal, other small positive changes will start taking place within you and around you.

Schedule Time for You

This is a BIG ONE for me. If you don't take time to refill your well, you will be no good to anyone else. Overcommitting to others, saying yes when you want to say no, and putting yourself last will only leave you pissed off, resentful, and angry. I know from experience the toll neglecting yourself takes on your health, your relationships, and the quality of your life. You have to honor your needs first. You have to learn how to gracefully say no to people and situations that don't serve your well-being. This is how you reclaim your life. The more you give to yourself, the more generous and loving you'll be to your loved ones. Does this mean you say no to everything? No, of course not, but it does mean you are selective about what you say yes to… every day.

You can do small things that cost little or nothing to care for yourself so that you can refill and replenish your heart, mind, and soul. Some of my favorites include a luxurious bath with scented candles, bubbles, and a good book, taking Pilates classes, getting a facial, or taking a long walk outdoors. Scheduling time on a calendar to do whatever nourishes your soul is the best way to refill and replenish yourself. The time you set on your calendar is non-negotiable. Just as you wouldn't cancel a business meeting or any other obligation, you cannot cancel this time for yourself. Set aside time for yourself and stick to it. You will be amazed at how taking just a little bit of time for yourself works wonders in every area of your life!

You Are Never Alone

Because of the feelings that come with divorce, or any loss for that matter, like shame, guilt, fear, anger, and loneliness, many women have the tendency to hide away and suffer in silence. You are not meant to do life alone or without support, and you are certainly not here to suffer. Healing requires a willingness to be vulnerable, to be open and honest and to share your experience. Sharing how you feel with others is a way to make sense of what you know now and what you need to know to recover. Whether you find support in a counselor, a life coach, a spiritual teacher, or a support group, the important thing is to be willing to share openly and honestly and to ask for help when you need it.

When I finally realized the value of reaching out and sharing what was going on in my life with my family and closest friends, not only were they loving and supportive, but they gave me a safe place to share my feelings and they offered to help in any way they could. All of those years spent worrying about and fearing being judged by others seemed so silly and unnecessary. And that's the real kicker through a divorce; often the judgments we fear from others are the judgments we impose on ourselves.

People who love you and care about you want to help and they want to know what's going on in your life. Share with them. Be honest. Just as you would lend an ear to a friend or family member in need, so will your friends and family members lend an ear to you.

It's Your Time to Thrive in Life

What I know for sure in life is that when you view a major change as an opportunity, a new world opens up that was not visible before. Divorce gives you a chance to redefine and rediscover who *you* are and what *you* really want. You get a chance to do and live life on your own terms. No more comparing, no more beating yourself up, no more playing the victim. Change is inevitable. The loss is inevitable. But you have a choice. You can either let go or be dragged. When you take good care of yourself, truly love, accept, and trust yourself, and no longer need anyone or anything outside to *make* you happy, that's the best place you can ever be. My wish for you if you are facing a major life transition is that you let go and embrace this opportunity to get to know *you* so that you can experience a love that is unconditional and ever-present no matter what is going on in your life.

Divorce Marks the Beginning, Not the End

It's 2018 and I'm happily married to a wonderful and supportive man. My three kids are now young adults who are self-confident and thriving in life. I am a successful Celebrity Makeup Artist, Life Coach, Bestselling author and Host of my own show, *Michelle Phillips Beauty.*

I've never felt more alive, more at peace or more in love with my life than I do today. But, my life wasn't always so great. In fact, I went through hell and back to get where I am. It may sound strange, but I am grateful for the hell I went through because had I not experienced extreme fear, shame, low self-esteem, and more, I would not have taken the steps to learn how to truly love myself and create the life I lead now.

I feel as if I am an expert in going through a divorce because I did so more than once. What I finally learned was that in order to be happy in life, really happy, I needed to figure out how to be the love of my own life, and stop looking outside myself for love, acceptance, or to feel whole. The journey wasn't easy, but so worth it!

The first step in learning to love myself was to let go of the negative thoughts that continually ran through my head like, "You're not good enough," "you're not smart enough," and "you're not enough, period." I also had to let go of the people in my life who mirrored back to me exactly what I thought of myself. I needed to let go because holding on to the negativity emotionally and physically wasn't working. In fact, I was being dragged down, and dragged down hard!

I share my story to give you hope and reassurance that you are not broken, you are good enough, and you are absolutely lovable just as you are! You can not only "get through" your divorce, but you can thrive in ways you never imagined possible. Trust me, even if it seems impossible right now, you can heal, thrive and use your divorce as a springboard to create a new beginning for a fabulous life.

Michelle's Triumphant Turn Around

Michelle Phillips is a leading authority in the beauty industry and one of the most influential makeup artists in the entertainment industry. With over 25 years of experience, Michelle works with national television networks, on movie sets, with top photographers, and magazines in the business including *Swiss Vogue* and *Maxim Magazine*.

You may have seen Michelle on TV shows and Networks such as *HTV, HSN, CBS, NBC, FOX, Oxygen*, and *TLC* sharing her tips and techniques that have made her one of the most renowned beauty experts in the industry who has worked with celebrities such as Katie Couric, Colbie Caillat, Condoleezza Rice, Sigourney Weaver, Clint Eastwood, and Presidential Candidate Mitt Romney.

Michelle's Best-Selling book, *The Beauty Blueprint*, has opened up opportunities for Michelle to share her message on speaking tours with inspirational icons such as Wayne Dyer and Lousie Hay giving women around the globe powerful self-esteem tools of transformation; a transformation to not just look amazing but to BE amazing!

Reflection

One of the biggest things we can take away from Michelle's story is she did mirror work. Not only did she check in with self to see how she had attracted the pattern of men into her life but she learned to forgive herself and be kind to herself knowing that she did the best she could with the information she had at that time. So many times we are stuck in a rut and we beat ourselves up for not seeing the signs or staying in toxicity too long or the list goes on and on. These choices don't help us to heal and grow so when you find yourself doing this, STOP, take a step back, take a deep breath and forgive yourself, be kind to yourself and grateful that you have the opportunity to start again just as Michelle did.

Tell yourself in the mirror that *I love you, I really, really love you* and connect with the inner child within, so that inner child can finally receive the love it's been seeking. This will probably be uncomfortable at first but the more you do it the easier it gets. At this point you need to be your own cheerleader, tell yourself in front of the mirror positive things about yourself and eventually, your self-esteem will be brought to a level that will help you thrive instead of survive.

Chapter 10

THE GREAT AWAKENING

In the midst of movement and chaos,
keep stillness inside of you

—Deepak Chopra

When tragedy hits, it's easy to come unglued as your mind swirls around in confusion. The first thing to realize is that you can't control the chaos, you can only control your response to what is happening. You do this by separating yourself from the chaos and remembering that you are not the chaos. Take a pause, connect to your breath, and remember YOU are the calm within the storm. By calming your central nervous system, you will gain a moment of peace so you can think clearly. Ask yourself *What am I feeling right now? What is going on around me? And What do I need right now?* This will make it easier to navigate through the chaos. It's OK to prioritize yourself!

Everything that shows up in our life
is there to teach us something.

Most of us define how well we are by artificial criteria. So when chaos hits the first place our thought goes is, but *what about my time? This isn't part of my plan? How come this is happening to me?* Instead of looking at chaos as a derailment, try to ask yourself, *why has this shown up, what is it that I have to learn?*

Our mind is powerful and every thought that we have has the potential to come into form so it's crucial to connect within, that silent space, the more you practice, the easier it will become and as time goes on you will become more aware of your thoughts and you'll begin to choose them carefully just like your daily wardrobe.

Yes, life can throw us some strong curve balls but we are stronger than we think. When the challenge seems more than you can handle focus your attention on something new so your mind isn't focused on what's wrong.

Once you have done that connect to your higher power so you can surrender to what is and know that there are powers way greater than you working on your behalf, serving you, and guiding you in the midst of the storm.

Finding Courage in the Midst of the Storm

ALL I NEED IS AN UNSWEETENED, GREEN ICED TEA

'To Have and to Hold, for Better or for Worse, for Richer, or for Poorer, in Sickness and in HEALTH, .'

The Love of My Life was now gone.

I had let go of the man I loved—my first true love. "If you love something, set it free; if it comes back . . . yada, yada, yada" is what kept going through my head. I had just come out of a long relationship, one where our careers were taking us in different directions.

I had just moved to a big city to start a new job. I was not sure I could love again. But this tall, dark and handsome man named John in a bar swept me off my feet on the dance floor, literally, as we moved to the beat of salsa music. It was love at first sight. An instant chemistry. "Could this be love?" I thought.

As we walked off the dance floor, I gave him my name and number—something I had never done, especially with a stranger. But I was hoping for THE call; and without skipping a beat, he called the next day to ask me out. Dinners, movies, walks around town . . . we saw each other every day for weeks. It was a love connection—one you see in movies and pray to one day be a reality.

Eleven months to the day of the meeting on that dance floor, we were exchanging our wedding vows . . . "To Have and to Hold, for Better or for Worse, for Richer, or for Poorer, in Sickness and in HEALTH, . . ." I always imagined that these were promises we made to each other in front of our friends, family, and God, and thus we would keep them forever. Why else make a promise if you can't keep it? I could not imagine breaking such sacred vows, especially since my husband and I had talked at length about breaking the mold of our parents. Both of our parents had divorced when we were young. We wanted to be different. We knew many couples that had successful marriages. They were not perfect, but these husbands and wives had worked through the hard times, celebrated the good times and they had been married for years. We knew we could do the same.

Our marriage was like many, we had good days and bad days. We experienced loss of jobs, financial hardship, family drama, lack of communication, childbirth and other similar ups and downs. This was normal. No one had handed us a manual on how to have a perfect marriage. We always seemed to survive and move on to the next adventure, hoping that THAT issue would just go away.

After five years of marriage, we welcomed our first-born

son, Evan; and four and a half years later, our daughter Gage was born. Overall, both children were healthy, but they also had some health challenges. Our son was born with a cleft lip which had been diagnosed in utero at five months. Prior to Evan being born, we had met with countless doctors, speech therapists and feeding specialists to prepare for Evan's first surgery at three months old—one of many. Gage, on the other hand, was diagnosed with Sensory Integration Disorder, which is on the spectrum of Autism. It was mild, but she had her own unique obstacles to overcome anxiety and texture issues. As new parents, this was, of course, very overwhelming. I found myself trying to be strong for both John and me. Thankfully, I was blessed with an amazing mother by my side to help me through the many obstacles. She was always willing to travel to help with the kids. I was working full-time, going to school for my post-graduate degree and balancing all the appointments, plus trying to be a wife, mother and public servant in my community. "God will never give you more than you can handle," was the motto my mom had taught me growing up. I knew I had to have Faith to keep moving forward.

I had just turned 40 and was at the peak in every aspect of my life, or so I thought. My children were learning to cope with their challenges and overall, doing well. I was in the best shape I had ever been—I had been training for my first half marathon. I had just been promoted at work and had been tapped to run for higher political office. And my husband had surprised me with an all-black birthday bash and invited all my close friends. We danced the night away to the 80s music . . . I could not ask for anything more. Life finally seemed 'balanced' and it was good.

In Sickness and in Health

When everything seems to be going well, we sometimes forget to take care of ourselves. We get busy . . . life sometimes moves at warp speed. I was Super Woman and I was on a roll; well, I was Taz (aka Tasmanian Devil) and just did not have time to slow down for my annual mammogram. It could wait; work was busy, and sleep was a luxury. In fact, I was not feeling well but thought that I was just run down from working and running every day. I did not have time to be sick. Women are supposed to have it together. "Mommy, are your eyes orange from eating too many carrots?" my sweet boy Evan asked one morning as I rushed to get ready for work. "Oh, yes, sure son. But carrots are good for us and for our eyes, right?" I replied. He nodded his head in agreement and walked out of my bathroom. I had no idea what he was talking about.

As the weeks went on filled with late nights at work, I continued to feel run down. I was the breadwinner in the house and always felt a very heavy responsibility on my shoulder. I could not fail my family. They needed me. Evan was 7 and Gage was 3. Once they were in bed, I would go for a long run at night, then come home, snuggle in a blanket on the couch and start typing away on my laptop. That was my routine—that was my normal. But now I felt like I had the flu—aching body, nausea, fever, dehydration, extreme exhaustion, to name a few. I finally decided I needed to go in and see my family doctor.

"You have a virus that has attacked your liver," Dr. Cathy explained. "Your liver enzymes are beyond normal range." "We will need to monitor your liver enzymes daily or admit you into the hospital," Dr. Cathy continued. "I don't have time to be sick!" I exclaimed. I immediately called my mom and was so glad she was only an hour flight away (and a nurse).

For the next two months, I continued to go to work but was only able to come straight home to rest while my mom helped John with the kids. I was so thankful for the family support. But I needed to get better to resume my role as mother, wife, career woman, public servant and everything in between. I had no grace for myself with so many hats to wear.

It was now May and I was feeling restless. The monotonous routine of work and sleep was getting old. I was dying to get back to the gym; I yearned to run. But I needed clearance from my doctor. As I daydreamed of running again, the phone rang. It was Dr. Cathy. "Hello?" I answered with anxiety in my voice. "Your liver enzymes are normalizing. You are definitely on the path to recovery," she explained. "Can I start working out again?" I asked. "Absolutely!" Dr. Cathy exclaimed. And on that note, I was out the door for a short, slow jog.

Struck by the C Word

Two days later, I went to the gym attempting to lift weights trying to regain my strength. My mom had returned to her hometown, and I had waited for the kids to go to bed before going to work out. I returned home from the gym and changed into my pajamas; took out my laptop and sat on the couch to finish some work. I wanted to finish early as the next day was Evan's field day at school and I was glad to be healthy enough to be a parent volunteer. I started to type an e-mail response when I suddenly felt sore in my upper body. I stopped to stretch my arms and gently massaged the upper area between my right breast and my collarbone. As I continued to massage the area, I felt a hard mass above my right breast. I knew I had missed my mammogram 6 months earlier; but what could it be? I continued to feel the knot. It was only on the right and not on the left. Was it a bruise? An out-of-place bone? Did I hit myself and not remember? I had no answers to these questions. I just knew that this lump was foreign to my body.

It was now midnight and I had been poking at the mass for what seemed like hours, speculating what it could be and making the area sore and red from the pressure. I decided I should wake up John. "Hey, sorry to wake you," I whispered. "But can you please feel this knot?" I gently grabbed his hand and placed it on the lump. "I don't know what it is," he said as he rubbed the knot. "Just have it checked out tomorrow," he said as he turned over to go to sleep. I crawled into bed next to him hoping I could get some sleep. But instead, laid awake wondering what the knot could be and thinking I could get it checked out next week. It could wait; I was sure it was not anything urgent and I did not want to miss Evan's field day.

Morning came sooner than I expected, and it was time to get kids up and out the door for school. "Mom, are you ready for field day!" Evan exclaimed with excitement as he ran into my bedroom. "Of course," I replied with a tired smile on my face. "I can't wait." As he ran out the door to grab his backpack, I grabbed my cell phone. Scrolling thru my e-mails, I saw one from an old co-worker, Pam. The subject line read: "Celebration of Life" and my heart dropped. One of our co-workers, Rudy, had died from stomach cancer. I had no idea he was sick. As I read and re-read the e-mail, I could not help but think of my knot. As much as I had prayed that I would wake up and it would be gone, it remained in the same spot—hard, big, out of place. What if this mass was cancer? It was in that moment that I knew I had to get it checked out ASAP. I would have to miss Evan's field day.

I rushed out the door to take the kids to school. As I sat in the school parking lot, I sent a text message to my OB-GYN, Dr. Rachel. "I need to see you ASAP. I have a lump on the top part of my right breast," I typed frantically. She immediately responded and asked that I meet her in ten minutes. I did not call John nor my mom. The only things racing through my head on my way to her office was the fact that I had missed my mammogram, Rudy's passing from cancer and the fear that my knot could be cancer. *Prepare for the worst and pray for the best,* I kept thinking.

"It's probably just a cyst," she said as I followed her to the examining room. She quickly numbed the area and inserted a large needle as I lay there feeling some relief that it might just be a cyst. Or was it? As I caught a look at her eyes, they seemed confused. "What's wrong?" I asked. "Hmmm, the needle is not going in," she said. "The mass is hard. It doesn't seem to be a cyst," she continued. "When was your last mammogram?" she asked. "It's been a year and a half," I answered. "I have been so diligent with annual mammograms since I was 35, but just got busy." "Let's see if we can get you in across the hall," Dr. Rachel proceeded in a calm yet scared tone in her voice. My heart was in my stomach. Something was not right. *Prepare for the worst and pray for the best,* I continued to repeat in my head.

Within minutes, I was in a room having a mammogram. Dr. Rachel said she needed to head to the hospital, across the street, to check on a patient and would be right back to check on me. I was feeling overwhelmed and scared. My mammogram was done and I was asked to sit in the waiting room for the radiologist to review the results. The wait seemed like forever and I was thankful Dr. Rachel returned. We sat there together when the radiologist came out to say I needed to have a needle biopsy immediately. The mass looked suspicious and she was concerned; and because it was Friday, if she could get the specimen to the lab early that afternoon, we could have results by Monday.

The radiologist said it would take a few minutes to get everything ready for the biopsy and asked if I wanted to notify my family. What could they do? I opted to not call anyone. Dr. Rachel said she would stay with me and hold my hand as the biopsy could be painful. And painful it was each time the needle clicked to take a specimen of the 2.5 cm mass in my breast—10 clicks to be exact. When she was done, she bandaged me up and told me that it was likely cancerous. She wanted to be honest with me and I appreciated it; well, kind of. I sat there without any emotion. I had just put my family through several months of craziness with my liver illness. They were all so happy I was finally healthy and running at full speed. How was I now supposed to tell them that I may have cancer? What was wrong with me? Had I failed myself and my family by missing my mammogram? What had I done to cause this? I was a young, healthy woman. I ate healthy and worked out daily. I was too busy to be sick. I wanted to get back to being normal.

Monday could not come fast enough. I waited all day for the call from Dr. Rachel and it finally came late that afternoon. Without hesitation, I rushed to her office. "You have invasive breast cancer," she said. "It's Triple Negative—a pretty aggressive type of breast cancer. I am so sorry," she continued. "I can refer you to a great breast cancer surgeon." I am not sure I fully understood what she was saying as she spoke. It was as if she was speaking in a foreign language.

She had confirmed my greatest fear—I had cancer. Growing up, the only cancer in my family was thyroid cancer. My mom had been diagnosed and treated for it when I was a freshman in college. I was checked annually for this as I was at high risk. But now I had breast cancer . . . where had that come from? Why me? I was a healthy 41-year-old woman with two young children, a husband, and a mother to take care of. I was an only child. I was the breadwinner in my family. They all needed me.

I got in my car and started to drive, not really knowing where I was heading. As the feeling of being overwhelmed hit me, I pulled over and started to cry uncontrollably. The reality had somewhat set in . . . I HAVE BREAST CANCER! I sat there on the side of the road and gathered my thoughts and emotions. There were so many questions and not enough answers.

I arrived home clearly looking sad. I tried to smile to no avail. My kids were doing homework and John had just gotten home from work. "I am headed to the gym," John said as he walked away from me. "I saw the doctor today," I responded. "I have breast cancer. I'll have to go see a team of doctors soon to figure out what's next." As I continued to explain my meeting with Dr. Rachel, John proceeded to change into gym attire. He had no response to anything I was saying; he could not even bring himself to ask how I was feeling. I wanted to tell him about my emotional breakdown on the side of the road. But would it matter? Within minutes, he was out the door with no further conversation. I was devastated, hurt and alone. That was just the beginning.

I sat with the kids to have dinner then helped with their bedtime routine. John made it back from the gym almost two hours later then said he needed to go back to the office that night. And as quickly as he was home, he was gone again, without taking a minute to ask me how I was feeling or even giving me a hug. I stood in our bedroom thinking 'I need to be strong.' Maybe he thought I was fine? Maybe he did not know what to ask or what to say? I didn't blame him for being distant and non-present. This was not easy news to digest. Maybe he was scared—I was sure. But I needed him to just hold me and let me know I was not on this journey alone; I needed a shoulder to cry on.

That night, after tucking the kids in bed, I lay next to my mom in her bed. My mom and I have always had a close, yet emotionally distant connection. She was a single mom, working full-time and going to school to give me the life she never had. I had thrived in life because of her. Yet, I rarely ever showed my mom my emotions and vice versa. We were two outwardly strong women. But that night as I lay in her bed, I could not help but show her a side of me that she had never really seen—one of fear. "Do people die from this—you know, triple negative breast cancer," I asked her as my voice shivered. My mom had recently retired as a nurse practitioner in women's health. "They do," she said softly. "But that is not an option. We will get through this. We can go anywhere in the world to get the best treatment."

I put my head on her chest as tears slowly rolled down my cheeks. I just wanted to go to sleep. This had to be a bad dream. But unfortunately, it was not a dream (or a nightmare). I woke up to a text message from Dr. Rachel with the name of the breast surgeon (Dr. Rao) that she highly recommended. I needed to call and get on her schedule ASAP. This shit was real!

I had come to the conclusion, in my head, that I would walk in and just tell Dr. Rao to remove both breasts. I did not need them. If that was an option, then just take them. Up until now, I had not said anything to the kids. I was so afraid of telling them I had cancer, specifically our son. Gage was too young to understand. But Evan would know mommy was sick and I was afraid it would affect him, especially if I lost my hair to chemotherapy. Oh, my hair! I was so afraid of losing my long, curly brown hair! That was my trademark—everyone knew me by my hair. But would I need chemo? My mind raced every second of every day as I waited for my doctor's appointment.

Three weeks later, it was time to see Dr. Rao and my mom and John accompanied me, and I was so thankful to not be there alone. Dr. Rao was a beautiful Indian woman about 5'3". As she walked in, she was surrounded by a peaceful aura. I knew this was the right doctor for me. As she sat with us to go over my MRI and test results, she began to speak medical jargon, but quickly translated to easy terms we could all understand. She was very straightforward. "Your cancer is a very aggressive type of breast cancer. It is also very rare," she stated. "We will start with aggressive chemotherapy treatment and see how that works; then go from there," she continued in a soft and patient voice. It was as if I was the only patient she had that day—and I knew that was not the case, but was appreciative of her time and compassion. "We will have to start right away as this will be a very long process . . . at least a year," she said. "And the worst-case scenario is . . . well, *it could be fatal*. I just want to be honest with you."

It was all too much to process and I could see the sadness in John's eyes. My mom was in fighting, nurse mode. I was overwhelmed with information. "Do you think we can do it all in 6 months?" I asked. "A year seems really long. I am happy to shorten the timeline," I insisted. "No, sorry. With chemo and surgeries, this could be more than a year," Dr. Rao answered. With that, she was telling her nurse to find a date in her calendar for that week to have a port put in my chest where the chemotherapy would be administered, and my blood would be drawn from for lab work. Treatment would then start the following week. What?!?! "Wait, can you just remove both of my breasts? I am fine with that option and we can skip the chemo," I pleaded. "I'm sorry," Dr. Rao responded in a soft voice. "That is not an option at this time. You will need chemotherapy as this cancer is invasive and I am afraid it may have spread to other parts of your body." "Can we at least wait another week to start treatment?" I pleaded. "I would like to take a quick vacation with my family." Dr. Rao nodded in agreement.

The next day, I was getting my port surgically inserted into my chest; and two days later, we were all off to Myrtle Beach, a place I had never been. John loved the beach, as did the kids and my mom. I had never really been a beach person, even though I grew up 45 minutes from a very large beach resort area. But the truth is that I had never really taken the time to enjoy the beach. I was excited to get away—there was no better time than the present. While I could not actually enjoy the water due to my fresh incision, I was looking forward to listening to the sounds of the Atlantic Ocean and feeling the warm sand between my toes. When you are told that your life may be short, the things you did not think you liked suddenly become appealing. I needed to live in the PRESENT.

The week seemed to go by quickly. I sat on the balcony of the hotel room watching the kids play at the beach and in the pool. John and I had also made some time to walk on the beach at night. It was nice to have my mom with us to watch the kids. I attempted to tell John about my fears and asked how he was feeling. With a glazed and sad look in his eyes, he said he did not want to talk about it. I craved conversation with my husband; I was dying for a hug. I held his hand as we walked on the beach and prayed for our relationship.

We returned home from our relaxing trip and chemotherapy began within days. I was about to embark on a long journey that included eight rounds of chemo over a 16-week period—infusions were every other week—followed by surgery. Day 1 of treatment was definitely the hardest; yet I'm not sure the second, third, or last was any easier. My blog entry read as follows:

> Day 1: Today was a big day—the start of a chapter in my life I only plan to do once. My mom made me a good breakfast and my son sat by my side. He looked at me and said, "I am excited today!" I sat there and thought to myself 'that's interesting because I'm scared and anxious.' I asked Evan why he was excited. He then said, with a huge smile on his face, "because today you start chemo and that's the medicine that is going to get you better soon." Wow! He had the right attitude. I smiled back and said, "that's right; my healing begins today." And with that positive attitude, my mom, husband, and I headed out for Chemo Treatment #1, only making a quick stop for a venti unsweetened, green iced tea from Starbucks.

During those 16 weeks, friends and neighbors took the time to bring us meals. Not a single day went by that our family was not taken care of with meals, treats, gifts for the kids, or some other generous gesture. Many times, friends stopped by just to bring me the drink that always made me feel better—a venti unsweetened, green iced tea from Starbucks. By the second chemo treatment, my body started to wear down and my energy level was low. My mom was taking care of me and the kids and that was a full-time job in itself. John would drive me to treatment and stay the day with me; but as soon as we got home, he would leave for work. On non-treatment days, he would come home from work late, turn around and go to the gym for several hours then return to work; or he would just stay and work all night. At first, I figured he was just really busy at work. Then I started to realize that he simply did not want to be home. He didn't want to be part of this journey.

"Do you think you can come home early today?" I pleaded with John on the phone one afternoon. "I would really appreciate it if you could be here to greet people when they bring dinner and thank them personally," I continued. "They always ask how you are doing." "Sorry, honey . . . I have to work," he replied, time and time again. "Well can you at least come home early and help with the kids?" I would ask of John. I simply wanted him home; the kids wanted him home. And my mom needed a break. I knew it was not easy for her to watch her only daughter deteriorating from chemo. She was doing whatever she could to keep me strong and healthy.

I also missed quality time with my husband. I needed a hug, a kiss on the forehead, my hand to be held. I missed sitting on the couch and watching a movie or football game. All the things we used to do together suddenly became a thing of the past. We were roommates at best. In my mind I was not dead; I was simply 'down' for a while. I knew we would get through this, but we needed to do it together. *In sickness and in health* . . . It was not as if I had asked to be a part of this "C" club.

As my chemotherapy treatments came to an end, it was now time for surgery. I would have to wait six weeks for my body to be healthy enough after the last chemo treatment so that I could withstand a 13-hour surgery (double mastectomy and reconstruction). John and I had briefly talked about the options and he had assured me he would love me with or without breasts. I just did not want to go through this hell again as I opted to remove both breasts and use my own abdominal tissue to reconstruct new breasts.

At the end of six weeks, it was time for my big surgery. But ten minutes before surgery was to begin, I was told my liver enzymes were elevated and my body could not withstand a 13-hour surgery. Over the span of three years, I would have seven surgeries, all with multiple hospital night stays and some even with nights in ICU. John came to see me every day but only stayed 1 night after much pleading and begging. I wanted my mom to have a break and simply wanted my husband by my side. That one night ended in tears after he left to pick up dinner for himself and brought me nothing, not even a venti unsweetened, green iced tea from Starbucks. He sat on the couch the nurse had prepared for him and watched movies on his tablet. It was as if I did not exist.

Keeping the Faith

Day after day and night after night, I prayed for God to heal me; and regardless of how I felt, I never stopped going to church. However, the stronger my faith became, the angrier John was with God. He was angry that God would do this to us, but I continued to explain to him that this was not God's doing. He was helping us every step of the way and I refused to lose my faith—I was chosen for this journey and we were not alone.

The one-year cancer journey Dr. Rao had originally prescribed quickly turned into two. It was now two years from the date I had found my mass; Dr. Rao had declared me cancer-free and assured me I would not need any additional treatment. Thank the Lord—our prayers had been answered! But I was starting to feel the side effects of everything my body had gone thru. At the age of 43 now, I was 1 of many young women struck with early menopause, along with hot flashes, chemo brain, loss of sex drive, mood swings, joint pain, and so much more. I felt like I was falling apart. In the meantime,

John continued to work late, go to the gym for hours and simply avoid being home. What was I doing wrong? I was now cancer-free and he still did not want to be around me. We had not been on a date since I was diagnosed, nor had he touched me intimately since then . . . not even a kiss. I resorted to daily prayer—for me and John.

A Statistic

For me, and for most people who get married, getting divorced was not in the plan and for me it was never an option. I simply never imagined it happening to us. Despite all the ups and downs, we had experienced, I loved John. We were not perfect, but we were not supposed to repeat what our parents had gone through. Plus, we had two beautiful children to think about.

John and I would hear stories of people getting divorced during their cancer journey. We knew it was not easy, but we vowed to get through these difficult times together and not be another statistic. Yet after every surgery and every treatment, I found us slowly drifting apart. I slept upright on the love seat in our living room, night after night because I could not lay on our bed. I used a walker in the middle of the night to go to the bathroom. 'What husband wants to see his wife suffer through cancer, chemo or a double mastectomy?' I thought. I convinced myself I just needed to give him space. I had no idea what he was thinking and could only imagine he had the same fear I did—that I would die.

The surgeries I endured left many scars, internally and externally, physically and emotionally. A part of my body that made me feel feminine was gone. Yes, they had been reconstructed but I had lost sensation and they did not look or feel the same. What would it be like to make love to John and have no feeling in my breasts? I had no idea as he had not touched me in what seemed like forever. "We can make love," I would tell him often. "I am afraid to hurt you or mess up what the doctors have done," he would reply. I missed John—his hugs, his kisses, his closeness. I just wanted everything to be normal. Yet I knew that we had to define a new normal and we were both not sure where to begin.

By now our kids were in counseling because they were both struggling with seeing me so ill. My daughter would act out like she was sick imitating me and wanting attention. My son fell into a depression. He had taken on the role of his dad when John was not around and worried about my wellbeing. They missed their mom; they missed our "normal" life and I did not blame them.

One day as John and I walked in to take the kids for counseling, Dr. Kennedy asked if she could meet with us. "How are you all doing?" she asked. "Fine," John quickly answered. "Why?" "Well, it is clear that your children are sad and we will work through it. But it is also clear that both of you are sad. Brianna—you have been through hell and back and I am not sure you are dealing with it. John—I know you are hurting. It is written all over your face," she continued. I sat there and sobbed with nothing to say. John looked confused. "I think you all should come to see me—together and individually. You need help healing," she explained. We both nodded our heads and walked out in complete silence.

After putting the kids to bed, John walked over to the love seat where I was getting ready to settle in for the night. He asked me if I needed anything. I shook my head. "What do you think about what the counselor said today?" I asked him. "I don't like how she made you cry," he replied. "You might need counseling, but I am fine." It was then that I knew that he was not willing to accept professional help for our marriage. I could not help but feel as though I had caused all the distance in our marriage. I felt guilty for having cancer. I knew I needed counseling to process my emotions and to grieve being sick; but more importantly, I knew we both needed help with our relationship.

I immediately started to see Dr. Kennedy on my own. I was doing it for me, for my marriage and for our kids. During one of my early sessions, we talked about the importance of taking time for ourselves. It was then that I knew I needed to get away to simply process everything I had been through over the last few years. I left her office and went home to search for places I could go to heal. As I searched online, I came across a site for a camp called First Descents (FD) and it mentioned cancer survivors. It was like that site was meant for me to see at that moment. I clicked to see what it was all about. Within minutes, I found myself applying for a camp. The next day, I received a call from FD letting me know there was one spot open in a camp starting the following week for cancer survivors over 40. By the end of the week, I was on a plane to Colorado for a weeklong camp with 15 other cancer survivors learning to embrace life and conquer our fears through rock climbing. It was truly one of the most amazing experiences of my life! I was surrounded by others that had walked (or were walking) in my shoes on their cancer journey. I made friendships for life and had finally felt like I would one day soon be normal again. I had found HOPE!

I returned from camp full of energy with a new perspective on life. I was ready to work on our marriage now that I was feeling better about me. John and the kids seemed excited to see me. Gage was turning five the next day and she wanted to show me the tie-dye t-shirts she had made for her friends with grandma. I was so happy to finally be home and feeling like we were on the path to recovery.

The next day was filled with fun, smiles, and laughter. Gage had her birthday party and it was a huge success. John and I were together like the days before cancer. Was the distance between us finally gone? Were we ready to move on? Had we found our new normal? I was ready to heal, embrace our family, move forward, and never look back. I was relishing the PRECIOUS PRESENT.

It was late when we got home from Gage's birthday party and the kids were exhausted. I, too, was ready for bed and hoped that maybe John and I could snuggle in bed, at the very least. I walked into the bathroom to change clothes. As I put on my pajamas and started to brush my teeth, John walked in. He stood and looked at me with a sadness in his eyes. "What's up?" I said. With hesitation in his voice, he replied: "I want a divorce." It was as if I was hearing the words "you have cancer" all over again. "I'm sorry—what did you say?" I exclaimed. "I want a divorce. Cancer has changed you and I am done," he replied. I fell to the floor, put my face in my hands and cried. This could not be happening! What had I missed? We were having fun just a few hours ago at Gage's birthday party, and now he was leaving me? He walked out of the bathroom and to the front door without looking back. I sat there and cried myself to sleep on the bathroom floor.

Love After Divorce

We had just finalized our divorce and that same lost feeling that came with being diagnosed with cancer was still there. It had taken on the face of divorce and a new title, single mom. Where had my 16-year marriage gone? What had happened to the man I loved? He was supposed to stand by my side. And here I was, a young single mother with two young children, medical bills and a body that did not feel like my own. What was I to do now? Why was I not able to be "strong" at this moment? The last thing on my mind was finding love again. I never imagined someone could love me with all the baggage I was carrying nor did I ever imagine loving someone again after the betrayal I had just experienced.

We had been separated for a year prior to finalizing our divorce and I needed to move on now that it was all real. I had begged him to come back home to no avail. The kids were sad and confused. They had just seen their mom go through cancer and feared I would die, and now their dad was gone—not just to work, but for good. For a few weeks, I cried and blamed myself for him leaving. I felt guilty—but for what? Why was I feeling bad, guilty and at fault? I just was not sure how to move on. The last year was a blur and I had survived because of the kids, my mom, my friends and especially my faith. I walked around like a zombie and there were days I did not want to live.

My friend Taylor had met her husband online ten years earlier. She kept urging me to create a profile and try online dating. I kept telling her there was no way I would find someone online; or if I did, they would meet me and run away once they saw my scars or learned of my baggage. "Just join for a few months," she kept telling me. "Go on a few dates, have lunch or dinner, enjoy adult conversation, make friends. You don't have to marry them." As we sat at my dining room table, she grabbed my laptop, created an online dating account for me and then drafted my profile. "Here, see what you think. It's simple yet intriguing." "I like it," I replied feeling excited yet scared. What kind of men would I meet? Would anyone want to go out with me? Ugh!! I was feeling overwhelmed. It was only a three-month subscription. It did not hurt to give it a try.

The hardest part for me was finding pictures to post on my profile. I did not consider myself a photogenic person nor did I think I was pretty. What were men looking for? I was so happy my long dark brown hair had grown back in by now, and I had options of wearing it naturally curly or blowing it out straight. But I was so self-conscious of how I looked; so critical of myself and so insecure. 'Oh well, I thought. "If they don't like me, they don't have to meet me." I was just not ready for any type of rejection. But if I did not give this a try, I knew I would regret it. I searched for pictures of myself on my phone, took a few new ones and posted them on my profile. Voila! I was online and feeling very exposed.

As I entered month 2 of my three-month subscription, I had been on a few dates with some nice men, some interesting men and some, well, not-to-be-seen again men. I will admit it was not easy, but it was fun to go out to dinner and have an adult conversation with someone of the opposite sex. That is all I really wanted. I was afraid to fall in love with anyone; I was afraid they would run away after seeing me naked.

At the end of my online subscription, I had decided that I would not continue dating. I was about to embark on a job change and that would require my undivided attention. I had taken a quick trip to California to see my friend Nancy on my way to a job interview in Washington. Despite telling myself I was done dating, I spent one night during those last three days of the subscription browsing the site to see if my 'match' was out there. It was 10:00 p.m. in California when I received a "wink." "Well, that's interesting," I whispered to myself. "Someone is flirting with me." Then I received a message telling me I had an e-mail in my inbox. I did not know why, but my heart began to race, as if I was about to meet the man of my dreams. I opened up the e-mail and it read "Hi. I'm Bruce." The short and sweet message had caught my attention—it was to the point and I liked that. This man was not trying to "sell" himself to me. My interest was now peaked and I clicked on his profile and took a quick glance before replying. As I scrolled through his pictures and read his bio, I immediately found him attractive. He had a cute goatee and beautiful blue eyes. I continued to scroll through his pictures trying to figure out whether or not I should respond. I really wanted to be off this dating site. Would this just be another "texting buddy" or failed date night? As I looked at his sparkling blue eyes in the pictures, I was mesmerized and could not pass up the opportunity to at least say hello. Plus, he had reached out first. Whether this led to a date, a relationship or simply a few e-mails or text messages, I had nothing to lose.

"Hi. I am Brianna. What do you do for a living?" I responded, thinking we might as well cut to the chase. Within minutes, a response came in— "What are you up to?" I started to tell him about my trip to California and then to Washington. We exchanged information about ourselves, our careers, children and favorite football teams. After about an hour or so, we decided we wanted to keep communicating more and exchanged phone numbers. I had butterflies in my stomach but did not want to get too excited too quickly.

As I landed in Washington for my job interview, he sent me a text message wishing me good luck. For weeks we texted back and forth due to our travel and kids' schedules, but no day went without some written communication. Knowing he was headed out of town, I picked up the phone and decided I would call to wish him a safe trip. "Hi. Just thought, we could chat a few minutes before you leave." I said. "Oh, I am so glad you called—it's so good to hear your voice," he responded. The sound of his sexy voice sent chills through my body and I was happy I had taken a bold step and just called. Why do we have to wait for the man to call us? He was about to board his flight and we quickly hung up. Within seconds, I received a text message from him telling me he was glad I had called and loved the sound of my voice. Yay! He called me every day he was out of town and when he made it back home, he asked me out on a date. We had been communicating for a month and we were both ready to meet in person.

"Where would you like to meet?" Bruce asked. "Let's keep it simple—burgers and beers. Sound good?" I replied. 'Perfect; you pick the place and I will meet you there," he said. While I had been on several dates, there was something different about this one. I could not put my finger on it, but I was over the moon excited to meet him and nervous, of course. I had picked one of my favorite burger joints halfway in distance from where we each lived, and we agreed to meet at 7:00 p.m.

I arrived a few minutes late; he was punctual and was sitting at a table with sunglasses on his head. "Do you always wear your sunglasses on your head?" I asked. "I do," he replied with a slight hesitation in his voice. I was nervous and did not know what to say. I sat down and ordered a beer and a burger. We talked for a few hours about life, kids, divorce, jobs, and whatever else came up in conversation. As we finished dinner, he took the check and paid. John had not taken me out to dinner or paid for a meal in years. It was so nice to go out with a real gentleman.

As he opened the door of the restaurant, we walked out and looked at each other. Neither one of us wanted the evening to end. "Do you want to take a walk?" he asked. "Yes, that would be nice," I replied. We locked arms and started to walk around the downtown area. We walked, talked and laughed for hours. It was as if we had known each other for years. "I love that gazebo," I said as we walked through one of my favorite areas of town. "I bet a lot of people get engaged there or even married." He smiled as we continued to walk. It was getting late and we both had to work the next day. He walked me to my car and looked up at the sky. "Check out the full moon," he said. "It is so beautiful and magnetic." As I looked up at the gorgeous moon, he looked into my eyes and asked if he could kiss me. "Yes, I would really like that," I whispered. He leaned in and gave me one of the most sensual kisses I have ever had. Our lips fit perfectly, and I did not want the kiss to end. The butterflies were in my stomach and I was on cloud 9. He opened my car door and gave me a quick kiss goodnight.

From that day forward, we talked and texted daily and saw each other when we did not have our kids. Bruce had been divorced for almost ten years and had three girls; I was still processing my divorce. Many of our conversations included me telling him what my ex-husband had done that day to upset me or one of the kids. Bruce would listen and assure me that things would get better with time. For months, we simply enjoyed each other's company. There was no pressure to take it to another level. He was very respectful of the fact that I wanted (and needed) to take things slow. Our time together included dinners, movies, bowling, listening to 1980s bands or simply sitting in front of a fire having a beer or glass of wine. Many of our conversations were at a Starbucks as he knew I loved venti unsweetened, green iced tea. I instantly felt comfortable in front of this man who wanted nothing more than to make me happy. I had been very honest with him from the beginning about my cancer and surgeries but was hesitant to show him that side of me. "We all have scars—small ones, big ones, inside and out," he had told me one night as we talked about my double mastectomy. "I see you—not your scars." I knew that if and when we were intimate, he would accept me no matter what.

We had now been seeing each other for about five months. He knew everything there was to know about me. He had even helped me unveil my love language(s). I had never had anyone explain this to me and had no idea I needed my "love tank" to be filled. What an amazing concept? Why don't all couples know this? Had I known my language and John's, maybe we could have worked things out? It was too late for me and John, but I was thankful Bruce was willing to have the conversation.

We had decided to take a trip together to Arizona to spend some quality time. We knew we would either enjoy each other's company or quickly get bored with one another. While my work consumed our mornings, our afternoons were filled with walks around the red rocks of Sedona, Arizona, and the small towns surrounding the city, visits to local breweries for beer tastings and an amazing helicopter ride. We talked and laughed together and simply enjoyed being with each other. He made me feel important and secure. It was a turning point in our relationship as we realized that two completely opposite people had fallen in love. I had found my "match."

Upon our return home, our relationship started to become even more serious. He wanted to meet my kids and I wanted to meet his girls. We talked about our futures and what it would look like if we were in each other's lives full-time. We shared our dreams and fears and found that we had a lot more in common than we had imagined. Our time together was precious, and we always enjoyed it when we were in each other's company. No matter what we did or where we went, we were laughing and smiling. I had found someone that genuinely loved me and made me happy. And yet, there were days I questioned if this was real or if this would last. I continued to fear failure as I blamed myself for my failed marriage. "It wasn't your fault," he would remind me on numerous occasions. "You did not ask for the divorce. He did."

As we approached our one-year dating anniversary, he asked me out on a date for that evening. I, of course, said yes. We had decided we would go back to where it all began—burgers and beers—and I could ask for nothing more. I was excited to be recreating the night we had met. He picked me up that night with a venti unsweetened, green iced tea from Starbucks in hand, opened my door to his truck and held my hand as we drove to the restaurant. This was his norm (bringing me my favorite tea and opening my doors) and I was blessed to have found such a gentleman and a man who loved me.

We talked and laughed all through dinner, we talked about the first night we had met. He thought he would never see me again until he kissed me; I remember being nervous and liking him the whole time we were together. As we finished dinner, he asked if I wanted to walk downtown like we had done on our first date. That sounded like a perfect plan. This time we walked holding hands. As we approached the gazebo, he asked if we could stop. He said he had never been and just wanted to take a look. "Do you think there is a full moon out tonight like there was on our first date," I whispered. "I don't know," he said. "It would be in that direction." I turned around to look in the direction he was pointing and was greeted by a quarter moon, beautiful nonetheless. As I turned back around to face him and tell him our magnetic full moon had not made it out that night, he was on one knee. "Will you marry me?" and before he could finish his question, my arms were hugging his neck so tight and I was leaning in to kiss him. I had not even noticed he was holding a ring in his hand. "Wait, I have a ring," he exclaimed. We both laughed as he put the beautiful diamond ring on my finger. The band was laced with diamonds in the shape of infinity signs all around. It was perfect! "Did you say yes?" he asked. "YES!" I exclaimed. I had found love after divorce (and cancer)!

Surviving and Thriving

I will admit that going through a divorce was worse than going through cancer. With cancer, there was a diagnosis, treatment plan and my journey was filled with hope. With divorce, I often felt like the sadness was never going away. The emotions were overwhelming, and the journey was rocky. But both were adventures that led me to where I am today; a place filled with love, good health, and happiness.

My son, Evan, asked me what I had learned from these recent life experiences (or opportunities, depending on how you look at them). As I started to answer, he said, "let me tell you what I think we all learned mom . . . " and I think he is spot on.

Love yourself . . .

Divorce lowered my self-confidence and my self-esteem because I allowed it to do so. While I had always heard "if you look good, you feel good," there were many days I could not bring myself to put on anything other than jeans, a t-shirt, and a baseball cap. One day, however, I had to put some effort into my attire for a meeting with my boss. I stepped out of my room and was greeted by numerous compliments from my two sweet kids. I looked at myself in the mirror and told myself I loved me. It was then that I realized only I had control of me, how I felt and how I looked. From that day forward, I made every effort to 'look good and feel good.' More importantly, it taught me that you must love you for who you are. Always remember to love yourself inside and out. You are beautiful!

Stay connected . . .

It truly took a village to get through those difficult times in our lives. When I was sick, friends and neighbors brought us meals, took the kids for play dates, came and sat with me during chemo, stayed at the hospital with me until I fell asleep, meditated with me, prayed with me and for me, and brought me venti unsweetened, green iced teas. "Mom, you have always been so strong and independent. But you found out that you needed people to help get us through some really tough times," Evan reminded me. He was so right. These life journeys had taught me to set my pride aside and accept help from the many people that cared. And still today, I have learned to lean on my village.

Stay positive . . .

I remember it like it was yesterday when Dr. Rao called to say, "You are cancer free! I know you worked hard with a healthy diet and lots of exercises. But more importantly, you had a positive attitude." It was not easy staying positive while fighting cancer. So many days I wanted to just give up; I did not want another dose of poison in my body. But I would look at my kids with smiles on their faces when I would get home from treatment and it was a reminder that I needed to do whatever it would take to get better.

Divorce was no different and staying positive was very difficult. I wallowed in sadness and self-pity; I blamed myself for John leaving and not fighting for our family. I allowed myself to literally reach rock bottom and felt complete hopelessness. I remember one day thinking 'enough is enough' and making myself find joy in the little things. Each day, I would find a little more joy and slowly, but surely, saw my light at the end of the long, dark tunnel. Finding those joys required having a positive attitude and not losing faith, and when I was happy and positive, so were my children. Together, we survived and learned to thrive.

I pray you find your inner beauty, focus on the good things in your life, surround yourself with people that love you, and that you always embrace the Precious Present . . . together we can all THRIVE.

Today, I am married to that amazing man that sent me the simple message— "Hi, I am Bruce." He is my complete opposite, yet my perfect "match." He loves me for who I am, just the way I am, and reminds me daily that I am beautiful. And every day, he comes home with a venti unsweetened, green iced tea from Starbucks in his hand. So, I am here to tell you that there IS life after Divorce (and Cancer). Life is a journey full of adventures, twists, and turns; it's your unique story and only you can decide what the next chapter in your story will be.

Brianna's Superhero Moment

Brianna Hinojosa is an accomplished lawyer, mother of two, and a cancer survivor. She is currently a senior patent attorney for Microsoft, with a B.S. in Electrical Engineering, a J.D., and an MBA. Since her survival from cancer and divorce, she has focused on telling her story in hopes of helping others on similar paths. She embraces every opportunity to speak or write about her experiences so that other women know they are not alone.

Brianna has adopted the motto "Fighting Pink. Living Purple."—pink for breast cancer and purple for all cancer survivors. She is currently working on her book that will outline her breast cancer journey and the healthy lifestyle she adopted during and after treatment. She hopes her book will serve as a resource for anyone diagnosed with cancer and provide practical guidance in areas of physical exercise, nutrition, mental, emotional, social and spiritual wellbeing. She believes everyone needs these 6 areas to be balanced to live a healthy lifestyle.

Brianna also enjoys being a public servant. She has served on Coppell City Council since 2005, with a short break to run for US Congress. She serves as chairman of the board for Las Colinas Medical Center and is a member of the board of the Coppell YMCA. She has recently married her "perfect match" and together they have five children.

Reflection

The two most important points that came out of Brianna's story is the importance of courage and having a supportive network.

There are times in our life when we are faced with an extreme challenge or loss of something and we have a choice at that moment, let fear cripple us or press into courage. When we choose fear it takes a toll on our health, our emotions, and our spirit. We were not born to live in Fear but rather in faith. So choose courage and squash your fears. Courage is the firmness of spirit that faces fear without retreating. This can be challenging when we live in a fearful world. But just as Brianna chose in her challenge, to be strong and courageous you can as well.

Her network of people helped to see her through her darkest days, her faith in a higher power, her inner will to survive, and the knowledge that God would make a way no matter what.

Chapter 11

HAPPY IS FOR REAL

My mission in life is not merely to survive, but to thrive; and to do so with some passion, some compassion, some humor, and some style.

—Maya Angelou

Almost all of the people I have run into are seeking happiness, but the problem is they are seeking it from outer sources, money, relationships, and materialistic objects. But happiness can't be found in those things, the secret to obtaining it is to know who you are. Who you are is the awareness of your perceptions, thoughts, and your choices. So the only way to obtain true lasting happiness is to be in touch with your soul.

When we buy into the thought of *when I have more money I will be happy, when I have a baby I will be happy, when I land the promotion I'll be happy, when I get married I'll be happy…* The reality is when those things happen we don't become happy; the end result is never as we imagined it to be. What you thought would make you happy doesn't because it doesn't feed your soul and you are still left empty inside.

Outside sources like the media tell us every day what it is to be successful and happy, how when we meet external goals that means we have arrived. But that is nothing but a false advertisement, so many people in life have reached their goals and they are still unhappy. How many times have you heard that money can't buy happiness? That's true it only magnifies the inner you. So if you are disconnected with self and empty the money will just reflect that. Yes, money makes the world go around but it ultimately can't buy YOU.

We have been told our entire lives that if we are beautiful, skinny, successful, famous, socially popular, and loved then we will be happy, but that's not the truth. Happiness can only be found from connecting within at a deep level, we are responsible for our own happiness! This is the most important journey you will ever experience, the journey to find out who you really are, an opportunity to find your truth.

So that means you will have to give yourself permission to put yourself first and work on yourself. An opportunity to be true to yourself and to say no to what feeds your history, and yes to what feeds your destiny. After all, what are you waiting for? The world is waiting for your awesomeness.

My Big Adventure

I'm Not Becoming a Statistic. Ever.

*"Every human being on this planet has their pain
and their heartache and it's up to all of us to
find our way back to light."*—Diana Nyad

Life is an adventure. Sometimes that unexpected adventure starts before we could ever be ready for it. For me, I was in 7 different foster homes by the time I was two years old. The eighth foster home took me in and fought to keep me for eight years until I was 10. Despite being with them for eight years, I knew this wasn't my biological family and it used to kill me. Watching other children get picked up by their moms and dads while I walked home alone just increased that feeling that I was alone.

When you don't feel like you belong anywhere you become dependent at a very young age. Sitting in my social worker's office one day, listening to conversations about me that I wasn't supposed to hear, I overheard someone say, "She's just a foster kid. Don't expect much." That stuck with me. Powerful words and I learned the word for that: statistic. Kids that grew up in the foster system were statistically less likely to be successful. I vowed to never EVER be a statistic.

Important moments come along that force us to make a choice. One day when I was 12 years old, my placement mother almost killed me. I had started to live with her when I was ten years old, and she and my stepfather had decided to start using me as a punching bag. On this particular day, she was angry because I didn't clean a pot properly (and this gets a little graphic, so brace yourself) and she grabbed me by the hair, smashed my face into a mirror, dragged me to the half bathroom and smacked my head off the porcelain sink and I fell to the floor. She sat on top of me, choking me, both hands around my throat. I thought I was going to die, there was blood everywhere. I had broken capillaries all around my eyes and on my cheeks and forehead. If I were to live through this moment I knew that I couldn't stay here anymore.

When she got off of me, I ran to my bedroom, grabbed the $18 that was saved under my mattress and I ran from that house as fast as I could. My mother was chasing me down the street trying to catch me, screaming that she would kill me if she got her hands on me again. I would never let her touch me again. It didn't matter that it meant becoming homeless, living on and off the streets until I was 18. I would not be a statistic.

You never know how cold it is until you sleep in a car in the winter, or under trees in the summer. The journey of being homeless took me through many adventures. I was chased out from under people's houses and garages so many times. I've stolen clothes off clothing lines. I've lived off waffles for a year and mini hot dogs for months and months and Chinese packaged noodles—oh the noodles. I've slept in closets, under beds, and behind couches so that my friends' parents wouldn't find me and make me sleep outside (yes, it happened. Adults had turned me out into the cold.).

That word "statistic" just kept coming back and I fought tooth and nail to make sure I kept going to school and finding food. I quit high school at the beginning of grade 10 so that I could support myself.

I was 16 and my guidance counselor was really sad. He felt he had failed me and it was mostly because he didn't know until that day what I had been going through all those years. He gave me a university entry level psychology book and told me to read it. I was against it, I didn't want it but he made me take it with me, and in my new apartment with almost zero furniture, this giant textbook sat on this little table I found outside on the curb waiting for me to pen it. Then one day I did open it and I read a little every day after working my secretarial job, and then more and more until I finished it. And I suddenly understood so much about some of the things that had happened in my life. I didn't know everything but it was a start. It was enough to get me to see that I had control over my life to some degree. I knew I would have to work on myself and I learned that the best way to learn anything is to teach it to someone else, and so began my coaching practice at the ripe age of 17 years old. You couldn't keep me away from the library if you tried, I was reading so much. You have to do the work on you before you can help others.

Suddenly people started coming to me out of nowhere, telling me their problems and I started giving out real solutions to really difficult situations, different ways to look at something, to take ownership, to not martyr ourselves or make ourselves victims of anything bad that has happened to us. Back in the day, people would be afraid to talk about self-help or seeing a "shrink." It's much different today in many ways.

I Attracted a Narcissist

> *"Don't try to win over the haters; you are not a jackass whisperer."*—Brene Brown

Through the years of dysfunction in my life and a lack of true role models, I attracted a narcissistic man into my life who I went onto marry.

If you have ever been married to a Narcissist then you will identify with their qualities. Narcissists want everyone to know what a victim they are, in their minds they never do anything wrong and they use techniques to change events and use arguments as a way to confuse you. They like to always be in control and they will use their lies and your faults to pick you apart slowly, causing you to question your own intelligence.

Slowly my life became dismembered and I became distant from my friends and family. I was feeling so hurt and alone, and a severe lack of love. I suffered from extreme confusion as my ex showed compassion to others but not to me. He was oh so charming that people started to think I was the problem when in reality I felt more like the victim.

It's Over

> *I realized that the life I was living was not the truth that I was."*—Iyanla Vanzant

It happens. You realize that the life you thought you would have forever with this forever person is done. You awaken to the truth and you realize that you need to get out of the toxic environment.

When it's over, some people will wonder why it's so hard for you to pick up the pieces. Others might be shocked at how easy it is for you to get on with your life. Secretly, in both scenarios, some days you can't get out of bed, some days you feel normal. Other days you can't stop crying. Or you can't stop smiling a stupid smile because if one more person asks you how you are you will literally start ugly-crying in public.

I put myself through eight very long years as I was trying to wrap my head around my swiftly failing and torturous marriage to someone who wasn't invested for whatever reasons. When I tried to leave the first time, I was a mess. He said awful things to me that I took personally and which felt remarkably like a kick to the privates. He wouldn't leave, I couldn't stay, I started to drink too much, I was mean and nasty, I was an emotional wreck. I was ruining relationships all around me. Self-sabotaging myself at every turn.

We divorced because we both agreed that it was the right thing to do. But it came with a price. I was lonely and I started seeing someone too soon, he was the worst possible person for me (too young, too free...loved me when I was strong, couldn't be near me when I was needy ...). When I first looked back at the choices I made, I would shudder in nothing short of disgust because I left a trail of bodies and bad impressions on everyone around me at that time. But time does heal, and I had to learn that it doesn't matter what others think.

Every choice we make serves as a lesson and we must forgive ourselves for being...human. I went back to that marriage against my better judgment, and put myself through eight more years of suffering. I didn't learn the lesson the first time. If you stayed in a toxic environment for too long, it's OK. Everyone has to make the decision to get out. But it only happens when you are ready and it doesn't mean once you learn the lesson that you won't make another bad choice. It means you can start making better ones and keep learning when you do make the wrong ones.

At the time of my writing this for you, it had been 32 months since I walked out on an 18.5-year relationship, 13.5 of which were married years. 10 of those 13 were among the worst of my life. One of the biggest lessons that I learned was there was nothing he could do to me that could outweigh what I did to myself emotionally. I have learned some remarkable lessons and I've learned them in some of the wildest ways, through the years of education: books, courses, mentoring, and coaching by some incredible people, and good old-fashioned hard-knocks. Strategies and techniques that have worked for me and the hundreds of people I've helped to guide on their journey in my lifetime, and all around timeless advice that you can fall back on no matter what you're going through.

The best part is that I'm still learning, but it's now with an openness that I never had before because I was too focused on the pain to notice that I was really in control of all of it the *entire* time. I still am. I am now in a position to begin to draw everything I want to me, have emotional control so that I'm not triggered by anything the way I used to be. I have found peace in my heart, I no longer look outside of myself for things to make me happy, and I feel like I can now see things from a bird's eye view and I get it. I can see the bigger picture. And this isn't fluffy inner peace stuff. I truly understand myself and I now know what I'm meant to do on this planet. It's taken me a long time to get here and I've worked very hard. That means that you can do it too.

I'm going to show you how to get through this very painful time in your life the only way I know how: through stories. So here we go... these are the lessons I've learned that I'm going to pass on to you. But first, take a deep breath...

Who Am I Now?

"I don't know how to do this but something inside me does."
—Paul Williams and Tracey Jackson

My marriage was a war zone with all the fighting and arguing and trying to make sense of nonsensical behavior, ripping through the lies, trying to make sense of something that made zero sense for 18 years, 3 months, and 25 days, this is what I knew for sure: I had no idea what the hell was going on. I knew the environment was toxic but that relationship changed me. It was an unhealthy relationship that changed me in many ways and I didn't see it coming. When I escaped from that pattern the landscape was different, the way I thought was different, I had more responsibility, more pressure, like real pressure now. When I settled into my new space: my condo was brand spanking new, white, lots of light, nothing but the beautiful energy around me ... this place was MINE! Mine and my children's. The negativity that had surrounded our lives was gone.

As I settled in, I was blind-sided by this thought: "Oh my God, who am I going to be now?" I had an idea of who I was, and I remembered who I was in my 20s. Now with a fresh start and this new path, I had to decide, who do I want to be now? I had to learn how to take risks again. That was something that I had loved to do.

How do I support my family since I had given up on that career I wanted?

How do I find out who I am?

Every decision I made served a purpose. I closed my eyes

and thanked that part of me who was protecting me, guarding me, doing my best to give me what I needed at the time. NO REGRETS. I absolutely do not regret staying home with my kids. I did it for them. It was the right decision for me to make at the time. Would I do it all over again? Yes, but I would have worked on my business or something that would allow me to contribute to the financial household. I was so busy with hobbies and painting and singing and playing guitar. I could have been spending my time making a real living. I knew better, I knew never to rely on another person for money, so why did I make the choices that I did? I lived the life I needed to live at the time and there is nothing wrong with that, it was time to forgive myself.

To move forward I had to learn to love myself, give myself a great deal of compassion and empathy and understand my choices. I was not a failure, but a work in progress. "Go take a deep breathe and have a talk with yourself in the mirror," is what I thought. "You are your best friend, which reflects in the mirror, so tell you that you have your back. For real, go do it. And promise yourself that you'll never turn your back on you again." I needed to love myself, and respect myself because my life truly depended on it.   I reminded myself that everything happens at the exact moment it's supposed to happen. I've got this.

How Do I Now Earn a Living?

"If not now, when?"—Eckhart Tolle

"My life is 100% in my own hands." This is what I was thinking when I was done crying from utter frustration about how I was going to get myself sorted and I peeled myself off the floor. Again. What do I want? What does *that* mean? A friend had said that to me. Simple, I thought: I know exactly what I don't want, so let's start there. Wrong. "Don't focus on what you don't want because that's exactly what you will draw to you," I thought. My whole focus was on trying not to screw up. But I knew if I was not careful with my thought process I would attract the very thing I didn't want, to go backwards instead of forwards. It was time to shift gears and focus only on what I wanted.

I got out a pen and paper and made a list. Three columns, no edits, money nor time was a factor in my choices for this list. Three columns side by side:

1. What are the things I love to do?

2. What skills do I have now?

3. What do people tell me I'm really great at?

Column #1 resembled what I was passionate about, everything that I love to do that brings me peace, joy, and soulful happiness. Column #2 were all the skills and training I had, not what I thought I may need (my talents), and Column #3 reflected what people had come to me for advice wise during my entire life. This is what I can do to serve the world, where I can make money.

Then I picked one thing from each column and put them together. Was this something I could do with my time, for money? The list gave me an idea of how I can serve the world, which I think is really the center of what brings me complete spiritual fulfillment. I knew I couldn't be daunted by the fact that other people are already doing my idea. Big whoop. If I stopped with that thought, I'd be dead in the street.

Fight for What You Want
The only reason ANYONE is successful is that they found a

way to infuse themselves into their work with 100% vulnerability, authenticity, and honesty, combined with compassion and empathy and some good old-fashioned drive. The secret sauce is...you! I realized I was what people wanted more of, how I have dealt with the process of life.

I made the same list about the type of man I want in my life, too. This time I'm not making the same mistakes as before. I'm not on a mission to *land a guy,* but I am very clear about what I want because I know my self-worth. I know what I have to offer and I know that I'm unique and loving. I'm a great friend and an awesome mama. And I'm funny. I'm the kind of partner you want because I know how to give without expectation. I want all those things in someone I choose to spend my time with, romantically and otherwise.

I got to thinking about my circle of friends: what kind of friends do I want? I make lists for everything. I know what I do want and, from experience, know what I absolutely don't want and I no longer settle for people I have to make excuses for. With absolute certainty, you can bet your ass that I'm going to make sure that I spend my time and energy wisely with people who want to be in my life and not people who tolerate me and you should do the same. If you have anyone in your circle who is sucking the life out of you, manage that. There's nothing wrong with outgrowing certain people and if you don't want to cut them out of your life, keep them at a distance. The healing process requires us to clear our space of negativity so that we can welcome in the things that help us to thrive!

Anything Is Possible. Now, How Do I Do That?

"Don't downgrade your dream to match your reality. Upgrade your faith to match your destiny." —Devon Franklin

One of the most important things that I needed to embrace is that I'm single, this means that I can do ANYTHING I want. *Anything.* The possibilities are endless. But there are a few things that need to happen:

1. I must believe I *deserve* what I want.

2. I must know what it *looks like,* closing my eyes I imagine myself getting the thing I want.

3. I must be GRATEFUL for what I have in my life and not focus on what is missing.

4. I have to take action to get what I want.

Visualization Exercise

Visualize it: close your eyes and think about something you've always wanted to do: what are you wearing in this image? Where are you? What does your hair look like? What is the look in your eyes like when you see yourself doing this thing you would love to do? Where is your happiness emanating from? Can you feel it? Try to locate the feeling in your body. The more you practice this exercise the easier it gets.

What you focus on becomes your reality. Think about it: the negative thoughts you have about your marriage and divorce are strong because you focus on them, you feed them, you give them life through visualization, and you become stuck. So if those negative thoughts are so strong they bind you, just imagine what your life would be like if you replaced them with positive visualizations every time a negative thought came in…you would completely transform your life. Completely. By visualizing what you want, and being as clear as you possibly can, your brain sees it, registers it as having already happened and with practice and repetition, you'll start to actually achieve it. Ideas will come, people will show up in your life, you'll start to make your move toward what you want in faster ways and before you know it, the things you want start to materialize. It happens.

Remember to practice gratitude for what you have, and all that shows up. Get *obsessed* with achieving your goals and creating the life of your dreams. And if for no other reason, do it just to see if you can. The *only* thing in your way…is YOU.

When I started my healing journey and visualization, I had to sit down with myself and seriously go through all of the things that made me who I thought I was: I had to sit with my belief system for starters and I had to ask myself what parts of that belonged to me and what was put on me by other people in my lifetime? Why do I feel the way I do? Is who I think I am, actually who I am? Am I really attached to certain thoughts and ways of thinking or can I give them back to the universe and create new ways and patterns of behavior for myself? As vulnerable as this made me feel at times, I knew that what ever I didn't deal with would find a way to rise to the top when adversity hit. Starting over meant developing a new identity by getting rid of what was no longer working and becoming a master at what would move me forward.

Make Yourself a HUGE Priority

> *"We cannot solve our problems with the same thinking we used in creating them."* —Albert Einstein

I sat and made another list, this time of the woman that I would love to be. I made two columns and in column #1, I wrote "Characteristics I need to have," and in column #2, "Characteristics I already have." I remember doing this when I was little, when I was living in the world without a mother figure. I give Oprah Winfrey credit she was my female role model. I needed someone to tell me or show me how to become the strong woman I needed to be. Thanks to watching many of her shows, this is how my list turned out: strong, vulnerable, fearless, bold, courageous, not a statistic, free, open-minded, compassionate, empathetic, honest, useful, generous, giving, always learning to be better, goes deep with relationships, takes care of herself, forgives, tries new things, smart, tenacious, decisive, loyal, and funny. Then I crossed off the things I already have in both columns, followed by circling the things left over in column #1, and that's what I worked on.

You Are Not a Victim. You Never Have Been and You Never Will Be

"We must be willing to let go of the life we planned so as to have the life that is waiting for us." —Joseph Campbell

I host an ongoing web series for women going through a divorce and I have interviewed 39 experts from all over the world to talk about how to pick up the pieces after massive adversity strikes and one of the healers I interviewed said to the audience, "...you have been victimized but you are not a victim."

Yes! We have gone through something powerfully difficult, but I feel like we have a responsibility to ourselves to make this the best life we can and to always be better than we were yesterday. As we strengthen, there will be a lineup of people who try to take us down. This is why it's important to find your "tribe," the one that encourages you and lifts you up instead of tares you down.

I am finally in a good place, through working on myself I have released from anger, and I'm no longer a victim nor entitled, I learned about self-love and forgiveness and I've worked for what I've wanted to achieve, got it and I'm still working. I'll never stop learning and growing and serving other people who are going through extreme hardship. I'm excited about the possibilities, about not knowing what's around the corner. I love that I can have loving relationships and give everything I've got despite what I've been through. I've got the most amazing girlfriends around me who are supportive and loving, strong and vulnerable, honest, wise and who keep me laughing until I can't stand, who protect me and help me when I need it and who are looking out for me. I'm blessed.

Being Present, in the Moment and Aware

"With every experience, you alone are painting your own canvas, thought by thought, choice by choice." —Oprah Winfrey

Remember, what you want is within reach, you just don't know how close it actually is, but it's there...you're only three feet from gold at every given moment. You have to prove that you can handle it by doing the work, you have to know that you want it, and you have to have the wisdom to see it when it comes to you, and lastly you have to be a good human: be generous, giving, loving, have gratitude, and look for ways to be useful even when you don't feel like it. Look for ways to help when it hurts you to do it (for example, with regard to money - if all you have on you is $10 and you see a homeless person who needs that $10 more than you do, either give them the money or buy them something to eat). Again, the way you talk to yourself *really* matters. Start paying attention to the words you use and stop saying anything negative. Shut that down. Replace any negative thought with a positive thought and thank yourself for trying to be protective but stop that noise in its tracks. Pay attention. Be present and at the moment all the time. Start working on yourself every day if you want a different life. Make it a priority, become obsessed. The good things that come to you will only match the work you've done on yourself, so keep going, and then keep going some more.

I have a morning meditation practice that sets my intention for the day. I have a gratitude journal where I write out a list of things I'm grateful for every single day. I send the people who I love but are bothering me to a calm place through imagery (I imagine myself sharing a space with them where we are calm and happy together, even though it may not be able to happen in real life.) I make my mindset my biggest priority in my life and I encourage you to do the same, it's life changing. If you need help find someone who has walked the path you're on and surrender to the work. If I can do it with what I've been through, so can you. I believe in you! It starts with that conversation in the mirror and a belief that you can have what you want in this life, the belief that you deserve it.

The Results Of Pushing Through

As a Personal Development Training Life Coach, motivational speaker and published author, Tanya-Marie Dubé hosts a web series called *Thriving After Divorce: Powerfully Reclaim Your Life and Turn Your Breakup Into Your Breakthrough!* and a podcast called *Thriving After Divorce Radio* geared to women who are going through divorce or separation and who need the fundamental building blocks to permanently overcome debilitating fears, self-limiting beliefs and feelings of victimization so they can thrive in both their personal and professional lives. She guides her clients to tap into their endless inner power and confidence to design a life they love and to fulfill their true purpose. Tanya-Marie has been coaching for

26 years and has a background in Social Psychology and is currently completing certification as a Tony Robbins Results Coach using the methodology and techniques from within *Strategic Intervention,* a program offered by Tony Robbins and Cloe Madanes at Robbins Madanes Training. She is also a weekly columnist for https://cla.world/. You can find out more at http://tanyadube.com.

Reflection

Wow, Tanya has transformed and raised herself from the wreckage of divorce. She made a decision to work on herself and invest in herself, taking control of the one thing she could control and that is her own mindset and well-being. When we take the steps necessary to heal we become better parents and eventually our kids start to thrive as well. But it takes time, it truly is a healing journey and it requires giving yourself permission to "put your oxygen mask on first."

Chapter 12

OVERCOMING ADVERSITY

If you change the way you look at things,
the things you look at change.

—Wayne Dyer

When adversity hits, you have a choice at how you want to look at your situation and exactly as you choose to see the adversity is exactly what it will be. For example, if you have a lack of money and you focus on that lack then the more lack will show up. Whereas if you see the opportunity in the challenge you will find a way to change your situation, attitude is everything.

Adversity causes us to expand and grow. We are programmed to think the negative so we need to retrain our brain to think differently because when we have a negative mindset it limits us from changing our situation. When experiencing adversity remember it's a time for self-discovery, a chance to check in with your internal gage. When you withdraw your attention from your situation it loses power over you.

REMEMBER: who you are is a spiritual being having a temporary human experience.

Taking Charge

Although I have never been married and divorced, I definitely know what it is like to overcome adversities. I may not understand exactly what you are going through but I want you to know you are not alone. If my story can help provide you the confidence and willpower to rise up from your position then I am grateful I was able to share my story.

I grew up in the Congo and life there had some beautiful moments and some painful ones. Although I don't remember all the events that took place, I definitely remember how I felt. The Congo had a sense of freedom, people felt rich indulging in the simple things like playing soccer with a stuffed garbage bag used as a ball and sticks as a goal. But there was also the sense of pain from seeing armed soldiers and my family being covered with fear. There are so many emotions I feel with the Congo. I was around 10 years old when we fled and the older I get the more it becomes a blur.

The fighting for power made the country crazy and we wanted to flee so we could experience a richer life, that's when we came to America. My father was forced to leave the

Congo and leave us behind so we then fled to join my Father. My Mom had to do so much alone; she is truly the strongest woman I have ever known. We first stopped at NYC and then joined my father in Dallas; there were a total of seven kids, my mother and father, all in a one-bedroom apartment. So, Texas is where we set our roots. But that's when things really became chaotic for my family.

In the Congo, I was known as the *Man of Tomorrow* and that troubled my father. Everything I touched I progressed in and that caused my father to set high expectations but when they weren't met to his standards abuse followed. I would like to think my Dad's intentions were good but his habits weren't healthy due to his own upbringing. Then there were cultural clashes that caused more abuse because my thoughts didn't align with my Father's thoughts and that came with a price. The more I gained my voice the stronger the abuse became to the point that I slept outside in extreme temperatures which landed me in the hospital and on meds after my father threw me out and said, "You are not part of this family," that was such a tough thing for a kid to hear. Move after move followed and I didn't know where my family was. There was so much dysfunction, I bought into the story that the problem was me, that's what happens when you get whipped and experience severe punishment not just on a physical level but on a verbal level. There was a time I remember when I was playing Play Station 2 and I went over my time, he unplugged the system and told me I was less than dirt. He smashed the gaming system and threw it at me and I just stood there in shock, my eyes were really big, he looked at me and I felt this rush of coldness, this freezing feeling on my face and as I touched it I realized there was blood everywhere, there was a huge gash in my face and he walked away. Before he left that night he came back and said, "I wish it would have crushed your whole skull," and I thought he was coming to apologize. All I wanted was a loving relationship with my father. That abuse carried over to my school where people laughed at me and bullied me because I had a bandaged head and a weird haircut due to it. Also, there were times that I smelt bad due to sleeping outside. It has taken me years of counseling to realize that it was not me that caused the abuse. The beginning of my life was filled with extreme fear and abuse.

Now you may be reading this and have experienced abuse, again, I don't know exactly how you feel but I can tell you abuse is wrong and it's not your fault, nobody deserves to be abused! It's so important when you finally set yourself free from the abuse, to not victimize yourself; reach out for help instead. Remember that misfortune is temporary, and the abuse doesn't define you, it's important to allow people to speak truth into your life and learn positive self-talk. The power of the mind dictates your life. There are still good people in this world and your life matters. I know today that what my Dad did to me was coming from a place of fear and I forgive him. It has taken me years and I have learned that even though life can be difficult, you don't have to go through it alone, we are designed for community. If it's just one person you find to lift you up and encourage you to be all that you can be then stay close to them. Anyone who thinks they can go through life alone, it's a matter of time before they crumble.

So despite fleeing the Congo, being abused, and ending up homeless, I decided to never give up on my dreams, one which was football. I never got to graduate from high school. I dropped out of High School and later obtained a GED. Life happened, and it became a bit challenging to receive a football scholarship because I wasn't playing and enrolled in High

School. Thankfully, I was offered a scholarship from Southern Nazarene University in Bethany, Oklahoma, they took a shot with me. I received my first offer to play Quarterback at the collegiate level. Now not only did I have a lack of academic achievements, I recently had surgery on my left and right knee. I was in a wheelchair during training camp, and I eventually found myself having to move back home at the end of the school semester because things didn't work out. While I was back in Plano, TX, the only thing on my mind was getting back on that field. So my days were mostly spent, working out, training, and working at the local sandwich shop because I had financial responsibilities to take care of. I went to combines after combines. I sent out emails after emails, nothing until finally, I made one right phone call which landed me my second opportunity to play Quarterback at the collegiate level. I was 19 years old at this point. I packed up all of my things (which didn't amount to much) jumped in a moving truck and started hauling my hopes and dreams six hours out west by myself.

I intentionally moved in two months earlier than everyone else. In an attempt to prove to myself and to my head Coach that I was serious about the opportunity I was given. I started a job working for the University in the admissions office, call center. After the first three days, I'd made more calls than I had the past three years. As time went on, I memorized more and more of the playbook, made enough money to provide for myself, and stayed in shape as I waited for the season to begin. Life has a funny way of just "happening." My coach pulled me aside one day and told me that the team was a bit short on scholarship money this fall. He then went on to explain that as a Quarterback, it was my duty to be a leader. As a leader, I had to make sacrifices for the betterment of the team. So,

I agreed to be a walk-on that Fall, which basically meant, I would receive no football scholarship and I would play for free, until the second semester. Whatever the team needed, that's what I was ready to be. Training camp was just that: training camp. Two weeks in, I collided helmets with the Nose Tackle as we both dove to recover a fumble. That concussion took me out of football, classes, any extra-curricular activities, and kept me in my bedroom with the lights off, Doctor's order. After my grades began to drop, I couldn't work, and the lack of scholarship started to really weigh on me, so I ended up going back home again to Plano, TX.

I started working with an organization that is very dear to my heart. I'd go as far as to say they saved my life, *City House,* a shelter for abused, neglected, and abandoned children and youth. I lived there as a child and some in my young adult years. Thankfully, they took me back as I tried to get back on my feet. After lots of counseling, mentorship, life-lessons talks and guidance, I decided I'd go back to school and just be a normal student. No more football. It was a tough call, but I decided it's what was best. I began checking out schools online and doing a whole lot of researching. Hoping to find another home.

I decided to visit a school that a buddy of mine recommended down in Waxahachie, TX. It wasn't too far from home but it was far enough that my folks from back home would have to call before they came to visit, the perfect distance, I thought. It was one of those nights where all the prospective students and incoming freshmen stayed the night on campus and got to see what it would be like to attend the school. Naturally, after all the school events ended, I started throwing the football around with my friend who accompanied me on the trip. People began to gather around. They were curious as to whom this random kid visiting the school was and how he learned to throw like that. I'd be lying if I told you I didn't miss Friday Night Lights at that moment. Soon after, a group of football players who were already attending the school came up to me and asked me about myself. They then told me they were actually going to have try-outs the very next day for folks who wanted a shot at the team. So, I figured why not, it would be a great way for me to get some closure.

That morning, my buddy and I drove back home, grabbed my football gear, and went on back to the school to try out for the team. I didn't care to make the team. This was my chance to finally just go out there and have fun, no pressure and no expectations, my last time to compete and play the game I love and then put away the cleats for good. It shouldn't have been such a shock to me that I threw that football better than I ever have. I had an absolute blast doing it too! From the other athletes to those watching, and the coaches, every-one was whispering and wondering "who is that kid?" I didn't care at all, I did what I was there to do. At the very end, we all got on one knee (standard practice for when the coach is speaking, especially in the south) around the head coach. He said something along the lines of "Gentlemen, on behalf of the University and our football organization, we'd like to thank you for coming out here and showcasing yourself for us. Two of our guys received a football scholarship from this same combine this time last year. So be hopeful, because that could be you. We will be in touch with you guys. Expect to hear from us in two weeks." I got up and went on about my business with a smile on my face, I had just gained the closure I needed. Later that night, the Quarterback coach sent me a text message saying "Ron we were very impressed with you today. We would like to offer you a scholarship to come and play Quarterback for us. We hope you will consider us in your recruiting process." I guess I wasn't done playing after all. To make a long story short, I decided to commit to the school, coach, and team and try to do the football thing one more time. Keep in mind, in between this school and the school out West, I briefly attended a community college in hopes to get a football scholarship there, but it didn't work out. So this made Southwestern Assemblies of God University my fourth school. This was it for me, I had to make this work or that was definitely going to be the last of it.

I moved to the school a little bit early. For two months, I was playing Quarterback for the school, preparing to double major and minor, delivering and making sandwiches at the local Jimmy John's sandwich shop, and I began traveling from time to time playing music.

I started to really get into singing and songwriting. Instantly there was a spark. Music began to call my name and I didn't want to answer it. I worked so hard and overcame so many obstacles to get to where I was in football. This time things were going smoothly. I would like to believe it all served a purpose. The relationships I built, the folks I had the pleasure of meeting, the stories I now cherish forever, and all of that, it all played a role.

After a lot of searching, I finally came to the realization that my true calling was music. So, at the end of the day, I walked away from the game. I didn't choose music, I ran from it. Instead, music chose me.

But just like football, music came with its own set of challenges but it also came with great opportunities as well. I remember it as if it were yesterday when in fact it was November 7, 2016, I realized I hadn't taken a day off. For about a year I got into my foster Mom's car and was driving from place to place, coffee shop to coffee shop; I went as far East as Philadelphia and as far West as Los Angeles, chasing the dream. I went from Texas to Las Angeles and back on $600 to play in as many places as I could. Then I got an urge to try out for *The Voice* so I went to Houston to try out. I woke up at 4:15 in the morning, drove four hours, got in line for four hours then sang for 45 seconds. I drove back disappointed having sacrificed everything for this huge NO but on the way to my hotel, I knew *The Voice* was going to Philadelphia so I booked a flight leaving for Pennsylvania. The same thing, woke up at 4:00 in the morning, stood in line and sang for 45 seconds, went back to my hotel and the same thing NO. So, later on, I drove to Nashville, ten hours straight by myself one way, I auditioned for *The Voice* a third time and I wasn't taking NO for an answer but they sent me home again with the same answer. There were a lot of people in the industry promising me a lot of things and people who thought they were in the industry were promising me things and nobody ever delivered.

I was so frustrated and hit a point where I decided from that moment forward that I was going to make the decisions that would best benefit me from a business and career standpoint. I shifted from fairy tale thinking to career based thinking. It was 2017 when I decided to get serious about music.

I had set an intention back on December 31, 2015, that if I was going to get serious about music, in 2016 I would experiment, in 2017 I would expand, and in 2018 I would explode, it's pretty cool how that has worked out. I started getting calls from shows and music competitions, record companies and management companies. I decided to go with *American Idol* because I like Katy Perry and then I imagined the level of wisdom and experience Lionel Richie has. I decided to just go and do my best and whatever happens; happens, it was a place of surrender. Every round I made, it was completed without expectations of making it. There were different rounds that I needed to go through before making it in front of the judges. I was enjoying the journey instead of forcing it. There is one time I cried on camera because I sang *Home* by Phillip Phillips, because for a long time when I was homeless and when I was bouncing around from different homes and shelters if you asked me what was home to me I couldn't picture anything. I didn't feel like I had a home for very long in my life and that's why I like that song, it's about people that make your home, not a physical location. So now wherever my son is at that's my home. I had to pull myself together for the interviews but it was from such a place of authenticity that caused me to cry I had to share the truth.

Never in a million years did I expect to come full circle from my original visit to America in NYC and end up back there for an audition on *American Idol*. Of all the cities they could have chosen for my audition they chose NYC, what are the chances of that? It was obviously designed to be that way. I feel like through *American Idol* it has opened my eyes to the reality of the music business through their mentorship. It was like boot camp, it taught me a lot that will ultimately improve my career in music and I have gained credibility. Anywhere I go out especially in the Dallas area people recognize me and I am extremely thankful for my experience and that I gained the courage after all the adversity I had been through to never give up on my dreams!

I hope my story has encouraged you. I would like for the world to know that sometimes the best thing you can do in life is just stick with it, that's your dreams. One of the greatest things that man possesses is his ability to choose. You can either choose to find the solutions or the problems. I highly recommend you focus your time and energy on the solutions. Take it from a guy who was 5"11' and at max 180 pounds. (The average NFL Quarterback is about 6'4" and 240 pounds.) You can fight for the things you want in life, even if it's not exactly what you're called to do. Be encouraged. You can achieve whatever you set your mind to. More times than not in life, the person keeping us from getting to where we need to be is the person we see in the mirror. Life is really hard at times and there are lots of obstacles we are inevitably going to face. Choose to not be one of them.

So where am I today? I have gained custody of my two younger brothers, ages 16 and 17 because they were being neglected. I am a father of a one-year-old boy, baby James and I'm now 22 years old, my music career is what has to support us all. There were times when I was working 25–35 performances in a month just to help us all survive and live in a three-bedroom apartment. There have been a lot of financial sacrifices made but seeing them with a smile on their face made it all worth it. Today, I am thriving instead of surviving.

So my final words of encouragement that I would like to leave you with are:

1. You are designed for greatness, the struggle can be an identity thing, don't identify yourself as struggling but rather that you are a fighter and an overcomer. You will then begin to approach your circumstances differently.

2. Invest in yourself and be excited about your opportunities instead of focusing on the obstacles. Look at every obstacle as an opportunity to grow. Life is like a track race, some people have a financial advantage and they start further ahead on the track than you. You may have

been abused and started the race a quarter of the way behind the starting line and that's not your fault, it's just life. But instead of thinking, "this sucks," get excited and say, "how cool of a story it would be if I end up winning this race." My life started to turn around not because my circumstance changed but my mindset changed. I stopped having a victim mindset, I no longer thought, "because abuse and homelessness happened to me, I'm owed," I started identifying myself as a winner and that's when things started to turn around in my life. I started to figure out and find ways to win!!

3. In regard to finances, when you hit a rock bottom point, realize that the things that make you happiest don't cost you anything. Find comfort in the positive, if you have health that's huge. Money can't buy life back! If you are alive and healthy then you are very capable of making money, it's a matter of figuring out the plan to make it. To get out of chaos there is nothing more important than planning. Time is the most important thing so if you have time and health it's just a matter of figuring out a solid plan.

4. Offer grace to yourself. Have patience and kindness for yourself. What you are going through is temporary and it's just a matter of time with the right plan that you will bounce back around. Sometimes you need to pat yourself on the back when you have the small victories, it's important that you become your biggest cheerleader. There is nobody who can encourage or discourage you better than you can.

5. When it comes to children, things are only as bad as you make them appear. Perspective is everything, it can

make or break a situation. It's our duty as parents to help our children understand things and we do that by showing them a proper perspective. It's ok to let your kids know that you disagree with your ex but explain that there is a correct and respectful way to disagree. It's ok to let your kids know you are struggling but with the right perspective. For example, if you are really broke and all you can afford to eat is roman noodles, instead of saying, "All we can eat is Roman noodles," buy a couple of different kinds of Roman noodles and say, "We have different kinds of Roman noodles to pick from." Give them a realistic brighter perspective.

6. You may be going through a court battle for custody of your kids, and yes that is a hard position to be in. But try to find the positive in your mind and remember there are parents that have lost their kids and will never see them again, and although you are going through a hard custody battle at least you know your children are alive and you will one day see them again. Try to count your blessings, it has always helped to turn things around in my life during some of my darkest times.

7. Try to plug into a higher power, whatever that may look like for you. There will come a point in life when you feel you have done all you know to do, it's very humbling, and that's when you have to trust there is a higher power that has your back, so release. When you have faith you gain a sense of peace. When you are going through all kinds of adversity and you feel the world around you is chaotic, all you want is a sense of peace. Life can be hard and sometimes break us down, you need something other than yourself to carry you because we can only do

so much on our own. You get to a point of exhaustion and you need something other than yourself to keep you going.

8. The best gift a person is given is the right to choose. You have the ability every day to choose to forgive, be happy, and what you want to do about your life. You can't control what's outside of you but you do have the ability to choose your thoughts and the best plan to execute. Also, choose to be love and you will eventually attract love.

Ron is Flying High

Singer-songwriter Ron Bultongez is living the American Dream. From growing up in the Democratic Republic of Congo to being named the "Hometown Hero" of Plano, TX and becoming a Top 24 Finalist on American Idol 2018, where he left Lionel Richie, Katy Perry, and Luke Bryan in awe of his voice. Ron's dreams have taken him far. His journey, depth, and spirit are evident in his smooth yet raspy vocals and his bluesy, soulful songwriting.

Chapter 13

TAKING BACK POWER

Life changing events can be very dramatic and disruptive, but they can also cause an awakening inside of us when we let them. The beauty is we get to choose to take a stand and thrive owning the truth that nothing less will do. Realizing that the things we had to go through were to bring us to a greater place, a place of growth and refining. An opportunity to surrender to what was so we can be open to what is and the new and exciting possibilities that are ahead, experiencing the flow of our journey.

This opportunity is for US to determine our dreams and the greatness that lies with inside of ourselves. An opportunity to unclutter our minds and make space for the magic that is about to happen.

Recently, I did this very thing, uncluttered my mind, took back my power, and unplugged after receiving a doctor report stating that I had a minor setback with my kidney. After a near death experience with reconstructive surgery and a blood clot, this is the last piece of news I wanted to receive. Although I was thriving in many areas of my life, I had a setback in the area of wellness due to lack of sleep and burning the candle at both ends. The Corporate America job, back-to-back radio shows, writing, acting and much more had caught up to me and it was time to put myself first. I started saying no to everything else and yes to my wellbeing. That's when I packed my bags, found childcare for my son and I set out on a journey to the Redwoods, a weekend I will forever cherish, *This Is Fifty Weekend* hosted by Sheri Salata and Nancy Hala. From the moment the shuttle pulled up to *1440 Multiversity* I was at ease. The doctor's report had slipped away from my mind and I was fully immersed in another layer of transformational healing, one deep within the Redwoods. The ambiance was spectacular, the people were like-minded and friendly, the food was exquisite, the service was outstanding and Sheri and Nancy treated us all as friends. We laughed, we cried, and at points, there was not a dry eye. We sang, we hiked, we grew through teachings and most important of all we became dream mates, there were hundreds of us all joined together to strengthen our *pillars of life* so that we could return home and write a new story.

"*Surrender Dawn,*" was the biggest message I walked away with, "*surrender and be open to new possibilities and really hone in on the state of your life. One without judgment, taking an observatory position and embrace the final changes needed to fully live the life of your dreams one with no barriers. An opportunity to fully immerse yourself in the authority that you are the CEO of your own life, an opportunity to write your own story, one with complete surrender to flow."*

Life had just unfolded so perfectly exactly as I needed at precisely the perfect moment with the Dream Camp opportunity and had I not had been connected with inside myself I would have missed one of the greatest opportunities for transformation. I have complete gratitude for *This Is Fifty Weekend* and the confirmation to surrender to flow.

Life is a journey and we always need to be sharpening our tools, learning, growing, and surrounding ourselves around people that lift us up and the reminder to make ourselves our #1 priority!

Chapter 14

THE GRAND TRANSFORMATION, THRIVING AFTER DIVORCE

Within all of us is a divine capacity to manifest
and attract all that we need and desire

—Wayne Dyer

As you have read from all of these stories it took courage to heal and the decision to put self, first, obtaining the tools and allowing self the time to heal, *this is what helps us to thrive*

after divorce.

In my case, I had tried so many different things to release myself from the victim mentality such as tap therapy, positive affirmations, visualization, reiki, chakra balancing, counseling, meditation, mindful living and juicing. I embodied self-help shows, podcasts, and books and I even kept a gratitude journal. All of those things worked together collectively towards my transformation but I still felt like a glass ceiling was left holding me back from my final dreams and desires. That's when I prayed and asked for guidance because I had done all that I knew to do. That's when Debbie Badamo showed up, I was at a business function that my friend Darcy convinced me to go to and as I worked my way to the back of the room, there was Debbie.

Now I had already known Debbie from previous functions but I never quite understood what she did. So, as the saying goes, when the student is ready, the teacher will appear, and Debbie did. I was so ready for my breakthrough and one of the amazing things she does is energy healing, now I'm not talking about your normal energy healing, I had already experienced a lot of that. I'm talking *body coding,* an opportunity to dump the memories stuck in my cellular structure, like a septic company coming in to pump out a tank as she muscle tested me for hidden heart walls and trapped hidden emotions, she was able to identify through her clinical studies and literature, the barriers that were holding me back. She then took a metal jagged ball and went from the top of my head and down my spine and said, "I am clearing Dawn of..." then we switched to the body coding book, a book of numbers, each number is designed to replace the negative coding that had just been pumped out of my body. Debbie, now using the same ball in the opposite direction from the base of my spine up to the top

of my head said, "I am now imputing.... Into Dawn's body."
From there I had homework to do, the final healing was up
to me and only as good as the amount of work I was willing
to put into my final transformation. I had to say the numbers
seven times over the course of five times a day repeatedly and
on top of that, I had to wear them on the left side of my body
in my bra with the numbers flowing vertically.

I know you are probably reading this and thinking, "This is
crazy." But is it? Throughout my nine-year journey, one of the
visions I had was to work at the Mind-Body Therapy Cancer
Center in Morristown, NJ, I always wanted to be *Patch Adams*
but God and the Universe had a different plan. Now if the
Center uses reiki (energy healing) to assist cancer patients in
their healing journey and everything is made up of energy
then why wouldn't body coding work? I like how Debbie
explains it, "It's like you are going to tune in a dial on a radio
to a country western station and you keep turning the dial
but all you hear is static or other stations, until finally, you
tune into country western music, well that's what energy is
like, fine-tuning your frequency to allow *FLOW* to happen."
Wow was she right, there were so many doors that I had been
waiting on to open and suddenly they started to open but this
time instead of pushing hard, the doors began to open with
ease, that's the difference when you line up your energetic frequency, you are now in the flow.

When you aren't in flow your conscious mind says you
want one thing but due to stuck past experiences, we self-sab-
otage what our conscious mind is seeking. So I sat down with
Debbie to discuss the shifts that she has seen in me during
the nine months that we have currently spent together on this
healing journey and here is what Debbie had to say.

There is the conscious mind and the subconscious mind and

the subconscious mind is always going to rule. There will be situations where you will have an attraction towards someone and you won't even understand why you have that attraction towards that kind of person. That's what happened with you Dawn, your past experiences and trauma with men caused you to repeat the pattern and marry an abusive man just as you had witnessed growing up. So even though you may have wanted a good guy, your subconscious mind knew the bad guy and it ruled. Now there may have been a part of your EGO mind that said, "I know he is abusive in nature, but I can change him." But there was another part of you that was attracted to your ex because that's what you were used to having in your life, it was generational, the abuse went all the way back to your family energy systems, back generations, there was a pattern that happened, this is what some people may refer to as generational curses. That is partly what you were experiencing Dawn, although your marital abuse was more verbal and your past with witnessing your parents fighting was more physical and yours sexual, your mind thought because it didn't look exactly the same way as what you grew up with, it was different but in reality it was the same, you just didn't recognize it because it looked different.

So you repeated the same pattern that you experienced in your past, that you didn't want because your subconscious mind which was based on your old belief system and past experiences overruled. So how did you make the shift? First, you had to recognize what you wanted and you became uncomfortable with the situation. You initially decided to stay in the discomfort of the marriage and eventually you made a choice to do something about it, you left your ex and moved 1,750 miles away to heal. You said positive affirmations during your healing process, but your subconscious mind didn't believe them, it was telling you that you were a liar, that you didn't believe it. So the affirmations were great but they were negated by your subconscious mind and that's why you became frustrated because the subconscious mind kept kicking it out because it didn't believe it. This is why there was still a glass ceiling over you, so I recommended an accelerated way to clear the result of the past emotions from your body.

The best way to explain it which is how I do with my clients is if you are sitting down and working on a computer, let's say you are looking for a recipe for a cake, you can put the word cake in Google but you'll get so much information it becomes overwhelming. Now if you put in I want a chocolate cake by Martha Stewart's best chocolate cake, it's going to take you right where you want to go. It's going to cut the time down for the search.

That's what you did Dawn, you narrowed down your healing time, you determined how you could change the discomfort, you prayed and then you were lead to me. If you would have kept looking at where the discomfort was and you kept talking about it you would have been doomed to repeat it because you were re-victimizing yourself. But you set your intention and you were committed to making the change. Once we connected I worked on clearing your subconscious mind. You have received through it a total transformative breakthrough. I helped you find and become your inner destiny, but you ultimately did the work, Dawn.

I started by looking for the energetic blocks that were keeping you from becoming the best at who you are. I asked your innate wisdom because I can guess all day long but I have to honor the fact that your body has more knowledge than I do. I asked your innate wisdom through muscle testing and I prayed for the wisdom on what questions to ask your body because the questions are so important. I asked your body certain questions and your body gave me the answers and through that wisdom,

I found where the blocks were. Just like when I spoke about the computer, your brain has a computer, the amygdala in the brain knows, it's all the stored memory; everything you have ever seen, smelt, tasted and experienced it is all in your brain. So when a memory pops up your body has an emotional response to that and what I asked you to do is go into that computer in your brain which can go back as far as in utero. How you were taught to express yourself and your belief system of how you were raised is what you decided to hide or express. So we took those blocked emotions, we found the age and neutralized the emotional effect that the trapped emotion had on your body. I neutralized down the governing meridian of your body, the spine. The amount of healing that someone requires varies per the individual and the number of blocks stuck in their memory. After each session, you reported that you felt lighter, so clearing took the heaviness off your body and allowed you the freedom to become your destiny.

There is also a component to the mind space of letting go. There were times when you were bogged down in accepting belief systems that other people gave you. It's similar to the time when you went to the doctor and they told you that you would never have another child. If you had bought into what the doctor said the chances would have been very small of you getting pregnant. In your case Dawn, you didn't feed into that with your son. Doctors told you that you couldn't have another child and through your own belief system, you showed them how you could. Same as with my work, I can only help someone to the level of what they will open their mind to in the way of new possibilities. When you came to me Dawn you were ready, willing and able to be healed and transformed. You did the work, you were hungry for your breakthrough and that combined with the body coding work, you have become your inner destiny. You made a decision to disrupt the family pattern, you decided to change, you knew what you wanted it to look like and you accepted personal responsibility for your life in a loving and forgiving space, a place of gratitude for what happened in your life and your childhood upbringing. You displayed a lot of courage, you re-evaluated yourself, you came from a place of gratitude and came to the place of peace with the things you didn't want to repeat, and you forgave yourself, and looked at yourself honestly. Then you set pure intentions and realized that which was your history and you decided to no longer re-victimize yourself. You broke down the barriers of your own belief system and you decided to release, forgive and no longer be a prisoner to yourself. You started to do things from a place of faith instead of fear. You got into the realm of miracles and started to feed your destiny instead of your history.

You have changed a lot, Dawn. You are an accomplished woman! It's a blessing that you've overcome so many things in your life. You now are integrated with who you are today. You have embodied your accomplishments instead of them being outside of you. You have now become all of those accomplishments. Your goals are now within you instead of you searching outside of yourself for what you wanted them to be. You are now FLOWING, you are grounded and rooted in what your dreams are and your destiny has become you!!

WOW, I cannot express the gratitude that I have for working with Debbie. I have officially crossed the line and I'm no longer standing behind the line and feeding my history. I crossed over and became a VICTOR.

I am so passionate about the work that Debbie does and how my life has been transformed that we have launched an invention together called *Cami-Soul*. Gone are the days of changing in the retail rooms looking around for my lost body coding numbers. Now they are safely tucked away inside the pocket of my dry and comfortable *Cami-Soul.*

I would have never in a million years guessed that my life would transform to the level it has but after almost a decade of working hard on myself and creating a magical life, I am filled with joy and gratitude that it has. I am honored to leave behind a great legacy for my two amazing kids.

Life is a canvas and we are the painters. What will your picture at the end of the day look like? Will it be one of chaos and judgment or will it be triumphant and transformed like the beautiful butterfly that is in the photo of this chapter? I pray that you find your way, and open to the possibilities that are available to you. Take a deep breath, step out in faith and know that God and the Universe have your back!!

15 easy steps to help you THRIVE instead of survive:

1. Take inventory of your life coming from a place of observation instead of judgment. Reflect back on what happened as a child or growing up that caused you to attract your ex into your life.

2. Pause and forgive yourself realizing that you did the best you could with the information you had at the time.

3. Get out a piece of paper and write down what you are grateful for at this moment, it will help take your mind off the chaos because what you focus on persists.

4. Plug into a support group, even if it's just one person who will lift you up and hold you accountable instead of assisting you in re-victimizing through the continuous chatter of your past story.

5. Write down what your dreams are, where do you see yourself if money and fear were not a blocking factor.

6. Make an action plan, steps on what you can do to help you advance day by day on your journey so you can one day fulfill your dreams and thrive.

7. Don't date; you are not ready, pause until you advance on your healing journey.

8. Get involved in something that makes you happy, take your mind off what isn't working and focus on what is.

9. Give yourself permission to put yourself first. Health and wellness are key when our bodies are strong our minds

are strong. We think clearly and have more energy to get through the challenges. Choose whole foods, anything that grows instead of dead foods, which are processed foods that make you sluggish.

10. Get moving, find a form of body movement that will keep you active. When you feel good about yourself you attract more good into your life, it's not about size or shape, it's about health.

11. Meditate, silence your mind and turn off the chatter. The answers you are looking for are within you but it's hard to hear when there is so much noise.

12. Mirror work—stand in front of a mirror each day and tell yourself something positive about yourself, for example, you are beautiful. This may feel uncomfortable at first but over time it will build up your self-esteem.

13. Understand that until you find pure love within you will never find love outside of you.

14. Surrender, to all things that are out of your control, with the understanding that everything that shows up in your life is there to teach you something.

15. Continuously check in with self and ask, Is what I'm doing or about to do feeding my history or is it feeding my destiny.

The biggest adventure you can take is
to live the life of your dreams

—Oprah Winfrey